Atrum
post
bellum
ex
libris
lux
·1920·

THE AMERICAN LIBRARY

10, RUE DU GÉNÉRAL CAMOU
75007 PARIS

Advance Acclaim for
If Your Adolescent Has an Eating Disorder

"*If Your Adolescent Has an Eating Disorder* is a powerful tool and 'must read' for parents trying to make some sense of the confusion surrounding these difficult illnesses. The case stories that are woven through the book wonderfully illuminate the realities of eating disorders while effectively embracing the reader with support and the reality that their family is not alone."

—Lynn S. Grefe, CEO, National Eating Disorders Association

"*If Your Adolescent Has an Eating Disorder* . . . truly will be a GREAT resource for parents! It addresses so many of the hard questions parents face like what to expect, getting the right treatment, and the realities of daily life with someone with an eating disorder. The book is real . . . it offers help and, most importantly, hope. As a parent of an adolescent who died from an eating disorder, I can honestly say that I needed so much more information than was available at the time, and I wish this book had been written five years ago. . . . I was especially impressed with the authors' ability to present very complicated material in a 'user-friendly' way. . . . They not only give parents, caregivers, and families the scientific information essential to understanding an eating disorder, they give practical information and advice from the professionals and the true 'experts'— parents—on how to cope with the multitude of issues that will follow the diagnosis."

—Kitty Westin, President, The Anna Westin Foundation

"This user-friendly, sensitive book is a masterful resource for parents and is written by the best there is—Dr. Walsh is a world leader in treating eating disorders."

—Kelly D. Brownell, PhD, *Professor and Chair, Department of Psychology, and Professor of Epidemiology and Public Health, Yale University; and Director, Yale Center for Eating and Weight Disorders*

"This work will be very helpful for the families of adolescents with eating disorders. It is clearly and well-written, informed by the latest research, and concise yet comprehensive. This is an important, highly valuable addition to the literature. I will recommend this to the families of all my adolescent patients."

—James E. Mitchell, MD, *The NRI/Lee A. Christoferson Professor and Chair of Clinical Neuroscience, and Chester Fritz Distinguished Professor, University of North Dakota School of Medicine and Health Sciences; and President, Neuropsychiatric Research Institute*

"Walsh and Cameron provide an intelligent companion for parents who want real information on the causes and complexities of eating disorders. Using real examples from parents . . . they translate the science into understandable explanations of all aspects of eating disorders . . . . Most importantly, they provide a roadmap for parents who are navigating the disorienting waters of finding appropriate treatment for their children—with clear information about what to expect as the illness unfolds and how best to advocate for and support a child in need."

—Cynthia M. Bulik, PhD, *William and Jeanne Jordan Distinguished Professor of Eating Disorders, Department of Psychiatry, Professor of Nutrition, School of Public Heath; and Director, UNC Eating Disorders Program, University of North Carolina at Chapel Hill*

The Annenberg Foundation Trust at Sunnylands' Adolescent Mental Health Initiative

Patrick Jamieson, PhD, *series editor*

Other books in the series

*If Your Adolescent Has Depression
or Bipolar Disorder (2005)*
Dwight L. Evans, MD, and Linda Wasmer Andrews

If Your Adolescent Has an Anxiety Disorder (2006)
Edna B. Foa, PhD, and Linda Wasmer Andrews

If Your Adolescent Has Schizophrenia (2006)
Raquel E. Gur, MD, PhD, and Ann Braden Johnson, PhD

If Your Adolescent Has an Eating Disorder

An Essential Resource for Parents

B. Timothy Walsh, MD, and V. L. Cameron

The Annenberg Foundation Trust at Sunnylands'
Adolescent Mental Health Initiative

OXFORD
UNIVERSITY PRESS

2005

OXFORD
UNIVERSITY PRESS

Oxford University Press, Inc., publishes works that
further Oxford University's objective of excellence
in research, scholarship, and education.

The Annenberg Foundation Trust at Sunnylands
The Annenberg Public Policy Center of the University of Pennsylvania
Oxford University Press

Oxford   New York
Auckland   Cape Town   Dar es Salaam   Hong Kong   Karachi
Kuala Lumpur   Madrid   Melbourne   Mexico City   Nairobi
New Delhi   Shanghai   Taipei   Toronto

With offices in
Argentina   Austria   Brazil   Chile   Czech Republic   France   Greece
Guatemala   Hungary   Italy   Japan   Poland   Portugal   Singapore
South Korea   Switzerland   Thailand   Turkey   Ukraine   Vietnam

Published by Oxford University Press, Inc.
198 Madison Avenue, New York, New York 10016
www.oup.com

Oxford is a registered trademark of Oxford University Press

Library of Congress Cataloging-in-Publication Data
Walsh, B. Timothy, 1946–
If your adolescent has an eating disorder : an essential resource for
parents / B. Timothy Walsh and V. L. Cameron.
    p. cm. — (Adolescent mental health initiative)
Includes bibliographical references and index.
ISBN-13: 978-0-19-518152-4 (cloth-13) ISBN-10: 0-19-518152-2 (cloth)
ISBN-13: 978-0-19-518153-1 (paper-13) ISBN-10: 0-19-518153-0 (pbk)
1. Eating disorders in adolescence—Popular works.
I. Cameron, V. L.   II. Title.   III. Series.
RJ506.E18W36 2005   616.85'26'00835—dc22   2005011596

9 8 7 6 5 4 3 2 1
Printed in the United States of America on acid-free paper

Contents

Foreword

The Adolescent Mental Health Initiative (AMHI) was created by The Annenberg Foundation Trust at Sunnylands to share with mental health professionals, parents, and adolescents the advances in treatment and prevention now available to adolescents with mental health disorders. The Initiative was made possible by the generosity and vision of Ambassadors Walter and Leonore Annenberg, and the project was administered through the Annenberg Public Policy Center of the University of Pennsylvania in partnership with the Oxford University Press.

The Initiative began in 2003 with the convening, in Philadelphia and New York, of seven scholarly commissions made up of over 150 leading psychiatrists and psychologists from around the country. Chaired by Drs. Edna B. Foa, Dwight L. Evans, B. Timothy Walsh, Martin E.P. Seligman, Raquel E. Gur, Charles P. O'Brien, and Herbert Hendin, these commissions were tasked with assessing the state of scientific research on the prevalent mental disorders whose onset occurs predominantly between the ages of 10 and 22. Their collective findings now appear in a book for mental health professionals and policy makers titled *Treating and Preventing Adolescent Mental Health Disorders*

(2005). As the first product of the Initiative, that book also identified a research agenda that would best advance our ability to prevent and treat these disorders, among them anxiety disorders, depression and bipolar disorder, eating disorders, substance abuse, and schizophrenia.

The second prong of the Initiative's three-part effort is a series of books, including this one, that are designed primarily for parents of adolescents with a specific mental health disorder. Drawing their scientific information largely from the AMHI professional volume, these "parent books" present each relevant commission's findings in an accessible way and in a voice that we believe will be both familiar and reassuring to parents and families of an adolescent-in-need. In addition, this series, which will be followed by another targeted for adolescent readers themselves, combines medical science with the practical wisdom of parents who have faced these illnesses in their own children.

The third part of the Sunnylands Adolescent Mental Health Initiative consists of two websites. The first, www.CopeCare Deal.org, addresses teens. The second, www.oup.com/us/ teenmentalhealth, provides updates to the medical community on matters discussed in *Treating and Preventing Adolescent Mental Health Disorders*, the AMHI professional book.

We hope that you find this volume, as one of the fruits of the Initiative, to be helpful and enlightening.

Patrick Jamieson, PhD
Series Editor
Adolescent Risk Communication Institute
Annenberg Public Policy Center
University of Pennsylvania
Philadelphia, PA

If Your Adolescent Has an
Eating Disorder

Chapter One

Introduction: Not Just a Diet

When Susan told her husband Ted that their daughter Vanessa had been diagnosed with anorexia nervosa, he was actually relieved. "In hindsight, it sounds terrible," she says. "But because our daughter was eating very little and had lost so much weight, we feared the worst. So when he heard 'eating disorder,' his reaction was to say, 'Fine. Now all we have to do is make her eat.' Unfortunately, we've since learned just how horrible eating disorders can be and how long it takes to recover from one."

Like Susan and Ted, many parents know very little about eating disorders, and when first learning their child has one, they may not know how to react. Some may think that their child can be easily "fixed" simply by forcing her or him to eat. Others may think their child has a deep-seated emotional problem that will take years of intensive therapy to uncover. Still others may wonder if their child's problem is just another "fad" diet spreading through the ranks of his or her friends. And still others may feel like Shirley did when she found out her daughter Jody had bulimia nervosa: "I felt immense shame—I could not believe that a daughter of *mine* would do such a thing to herself. You see, I thought bulimia was a choice. If one could choose to begin the behavior, then one could choose to end it as well. Due to the shame and the stigma—our culture reinforces this notion of "a spoiled white girl's choice"—it was difficult for me to admit to all but my closest friends what was happening within our family."

"I could not believe that a daughter of mine would do such a thing to herself."

This variety of reactions reflects the fact that the term *eating disorder*, even in the community of professionals who specialize in treating such disturbances, describes a broad spectrum of problems. Two eating disorders, anorexia nervosa and bulimia nervosa, are clearly defined and have been extensively studied. They are serious, potentially life-threatening illnesses that predominantly affect young females, but can also affect others regardless of age, gender, race, or economic background. In addition, eating disorder specialists recognize that many young people have significant eating problems that interfere with normal physical and emotional development, but are not quite full-blown anorexia nervosa or bulimia nervosa. And, as well, many more young people develop unusual eating habits and food preferences that are peculiar but transient and harmless, as Anne's experience with her daughter Charlotte demonstrates.

As a child, Charlotte had eaten everything put in front of her, but when she turned thirteen, she suddenly refused to eat anything except a certain few foods that didn't exactly create a balanced diet. Anne tried to encourage her to eat other things, but nothing else would do. If her favorite foods weren't on the menu (either at home or elsewhere), Charlotte preferred to go hungry.

A former ice skater who'd won numerous awards at amateur competitions, Anne had aspired to join a professional ice show but gave up her dream when she saw how other skaters starved themselves or used diuretics or laxatives to meet the required weight limit. To her, skating was something she loved doing, but not to the point where it might do physical harm. Having witnessed her former colleagues' unhealthy behaviors, she became concerned about Charlotte's food restrictions, and took her daughter to a physician who specialized in eating disorders. Upon hearing Anne's concerns, the doctor performed a blood test followed by a physical examination. Then, and most importantly (according to Anne), he had a long talk with Charlotte and advised Anne to do the same. In the end, neither doctor nor mother could find any physical or psychological evidence that Charlotte was experiencing anything other than a change in her tastes. She proved to be a self-assured, robust, healthy teenager who just happened to like only certain foods. Charlotte eventually went off to college, then got married and had kids of her own, who now frequently bedevil her with what they will or won't eat.

While the onset of eating disorders usually occurs around the start of, or soon after, puberty, not all teenagers who alter their eating habits should be immediately suspect. As parents know from having been teenagers themselves, adolescence is a turbulent time that brings with it added social and academic pressures as well as physiological changes. Consequently, a formerly voracious eater might suddenly become a picky one, an increase in school or extracurricular activities can cause kids to miss family meals, and all those "raging hormones" can make teenagers focus more on their appearance.

> . . . adolescence is a turbulent time that brings with it added social and academic pressures as well as physiological changes

Diane, whose daughter Megan is now recovering from anorexia nervosa, recalls, "When your daughter first goes on a diet, you always think, 'Well, okay, everybody diets.' I certainly did when I was young, mostly because all of my friends were doing it. That's why I didn't say anything to Megan when she went on a diet. She's really smart and I knew that, given time, she'd figure it all out and give up the dieting thing, too. Unfortunately, that wasn't the case and I now deeply regret not talking to her sooner."

As the previous illustrations demonstrate, the wide range of human food preferences and consumption can make the recognition of a serious eating disorder difficult. This is particularly true during adolescence, when kids require more energy to support their bodies' normal growth and development. According to a 2002 report from the Committee on Dietary Reference Intakes, Institute of Medicine, in Washington, DC, the number of calories girls need to eat increases between ages 9 and 19 by almost 50% and for boys, by 80%. Perhaps in part because of this dramatic biological imperative, combined with society's ever-changing notion of how one "should" look, it is common for teenagers to start dieting. These and other elements can create a fertile environment for the development of disordered eating, as the following statistics from the medical literature illustrate:

- A study published in 2001 found that among children in third grade, 26% of boys and 35% of girls reported wanting to lose weight, and 17% of boys and 24% of girls were dieting.

- As of 2002, 56% percent of ninth-grade females and 28% of ninth-grade males reported binge eating or engaging in one or more of the following to lose or control weight:

fasting or skipping meals, taking diet pills or laxatives, inducing vomiting, or smoking cigarettes.

• In 2001, almost two-thirds of female high school students and one-third of male students were trying to lose weight.

These numbers highlight the very high rates of concern about weight control among youngsters, and the strong wish, especially among girls, to lose weight. Fortunately, the most serious eating disorders are much less common. While there is substantial uncertainty about their prevalence, the general consensus among experts is that full-blown eating disorders occur in approximately 1% (anorexia nervosa) to 3% (bulimia nervosa) of women at some point during their lives, with the rates among men approximately one-tenth of those observed in women. And what about among teenagers? In this age group, the figures are not precise, but a report, from the Committee on Adolescence of the American Academy of Pediatrics in January 2003, estimated that as many as 0.5% of American teenage girls have anorexia nervosa, 1% to 5% have bulimia nervosa, and up to 10% of all cases of eating disorders occur in males.

More will be said later about how eating disorders are formally defined by experts and about how many young people develop them, but for now the key point we want to emphasize about the statistics on adolescents is this: All of these teenagers have a parent or parents who have had to face the impact of these disorders on their children's and on their own daily lives. They've all had questions about these illnesses—What are they? What causes them? What can make them go away? The scientific community of researchers on eating disorders has answers to these questions, but most of the answers are incomplete, and much remains to be discovered about the causes, treatments, and prevention of these illnesses. Indeed, if you are the parent of a child with or at risk for an eating disorder, you likely have many more questions about your child than are possible to answer conclusively at this time. Our aim in this book is to give you the best scientific information on eating disorders that can currently be provided and to give you a sense of what you will likely encounter as you go about getting help for your child. Clearly, we cannot answer all your questions, nor can a book stand in the place of actual professional evaluation and treatment. But we can help you understand what your adolescent is going through and what you as a parent can do to help him or her recover.

The scientific material presented here draws in large part from the findings of a 15-member Commission on Eating Disorders, chaired by the lead author of this book, that was part of the Adolescent Mental Health Initiative spearheaded in 2003 by the Annenberg Foundation Trust at Sunnylands to address the increasing prevalence of severe mental illness (e.g., depression, anxiety disorders, eating disorders, and other conditions) among our nation's young people. The book draws from other sources as well, most compellingly from parents who have faced these disorders in their own children. For a few of these parents, the struggle to save their children from the ravages of anorexia nervosa or bulimia nervosa was sadly lost. For others, the struggle continues to this day. And for still others, the struggle has been hard but ultimately triumphant. Regardless of outcome, they have all gone through something similar to what you're going through now, and they have agreed to be interviewed for this book in order to reach out and impart to you what they have learned about these disorders from ex-

The book draws from other sources as well, most compellingly from parents who have faced these disorders in their own children.

periences with their own kids. The same is true for the two people, now adults, whose recollections of having eating disorders as teens have also been included in the book. The names of all the people who spoke to us have been changed in order to protect their privacy, but the experiences they shared with us for this book are very real. Together they form something of "virtual support group," providing a wealth of practical wisdom and personal insights that we believe you'll find meaningful. We are exceedingly grateful to them for their courage and generosity in opening up their lives to us for this purpose.

Chapter Two

Understanding Eating Disorders: What They Are and What to Expect

Anorexia Nervosa

When Chelsey started skipping meals and isolating herself from family and friends, her parents began to worry. "As a young girl, she was always so outgoing," her mother Donna says. "She had lots of friends and was involved in all kinds of social activities. She was also high-achieving and a perfectionist. Everything had to be done just so and if something wasn't done exactly the way she thought it should be, she'd become distressed and do it over and over again until she got it right. This perfectionistic attitude spilled over into her drive to be thin. When my husband and I finally told her she needed to stop dieting, she became angry and defensive with us for interfering in her life. That really took us by surprise because she'd never spoken to us that way before. We later found out that she didn't just want to be thin, she wanted to be thinner than everyone else."

"This perfectionistic attitude spilled over into her drive to be thin."

Valerie noticed similar changes in her daughter Audra. "She became very withdrawn and secretive. She started acting as though there was some inner force driving her to keep moving and stay busy. She suddenly became very preoccupied and had a short attention span. As her physical condition deteriorated, she also became extremely short-tempered and her thinking was irrational at times. When her weight reached the critical stage, she even became violent."

Diane's first clue that something was wrong with Megan came when her daughter returned home after her first year away at college. "She was extremely thin, always cold, and looked unhealthy," Diane recalls. "Plus her relationship to food had completely changed. Before, she'd always loved food, she had celebrated it, but all that changed after she came back from school and it was clear she was seeing food in a different way. She suddenly agonized over what she could or couldn't eat, and grocery shopping turned into an exhausting ordeal because she had to calculate every calorie and fat gram. If the total amounted to more than she was willing to allow herself, she'd put the food back rather than adding it to the cart. Her healthy relationship with food had changed to an unhealthy one and trying to get her to eat anything became a nightmare."

Chelsey, Audra, and Megan were all exhibiting signs and symptoms of anorexia nervosa, a complex mental disorder that can cause a person to literally "waste away" due to an intense fear of being fat. Even when at a dangerously low weight, a teen can refer to herself as a "fat cow" because the disease distorts how people think about themselves.

Anorexia nervosa normally begins around the onset of puberty, and full-blown cases occur in about one in every 200 adolescents, with 90% to 95% of those teenagers being girls. Anorexia nervosa is one of the deadliest psychiatric disorders, with a mortality rate estimated at 0.56% per year, or approximately 5.6% per decade. That statistic is approximately 12 times higher than the annual death rate due to all causes of death among females between the ages 15 to 24 in the general population. Further discussion about the prevalence or frequency of anorexia nervosa appears later in this chapter, in the section, "How Common Are Eating Disorders in Adolescents?" (pp. 32–36).

By itself, the term *anorexia* actually means "loss of appetite." Virtually everyone has experienced anorexia: for example, "stomach flu" and a number of medications, like some types of chemotherapy drugs, can produce an aversion to food and cause weight loss. Those with the mental disorder "anorexia nervosa," however, do not have an aversion to food. In fact, they are almost always hungry and think about food constantly even as the disorder impels them to deny their bodies the fuel needed to function properly. This denial of the normal desire for food can even include going to great lengths to "protect" the disease, such as avoiding social occasions involving meals, trying to hide severe weight loss by wearing baggy clothes, or lying to family and friends about what they are or aren't eating.

"It's hard to believe that your own kid would lie right to your face," Diane says, "especially if they've never done it before. So

"It's hard to believe that your own kid would lie right to your face."

when they say they had a big lunch or ate dinner with a friend, you believe them. There's nothing to tell you you shouldn't. I mean, who wants to think their daughter is not only a liar but is purposely trying to starve herself to death?"

While many children in the throes of anorexia nervosa do wind up actually starving themselves to a critical point physically, few set out with such a mission in mind. The disease can often take hold because they start out feeling betrayed by their changing bodies. With the onset of puberty, a girl suddenly has to deal with a figure that is becoming round and curvy—with growing breasts, hips, buttocks, and thighs—which can make her feel extremely self-conscious and even distressed. Likewise, an adolescent boy who grows wider instead of taller might be the object of ridicule from his peers because his "baby fat" makes him look too much like "a girl." In our culture, a remarkably high percentage of both boys and girls are unhappy with their appearance. According to one study of sixth to eighth graders, 26% of girls and 22% of boys believed they were significantly overweight, and even higher fractions of girls and boys were trying to lose weight. The dissatisfaction with physical appearance suggested by such statistics, along with the mental and physical changes that accompany the onset of puberty, can trigger all kinds of disordered-eating behaviors in sensitive children who define their self-worth by how they look.

Additionally, when some kids do go on a diet and lose weight, they can become so intoxicated with praise from friends or relatives (e.g., "Wow, you look great! or "Man, that diet really worked, didn't it?") that they might think, "Well, if you think I look good now, just wait and see how good I look after I lose another ten pounds." Unfortunately, the more one becomes burdened with the drive to be thin or to maintain thinness, the more it can become an obsession. One adolescent even described herself as a "soldier" in the fight not to succumb to the enemy (hunger), with every second, every minute, and every hour of her life being driven by the need to win the "war" waged between her body and her need to control it.

Public awareness about anorexia nervosa has increased dramatically in the last few decades, in part because of the media's focus on celebrities with eating disorders. One of the earliest examples occurred in 1983, when Grammy Award-winning pop singer Karen Carpenter died of heart failure at the age of 32 as a result of the long-term effects of self-starvation, self-induced vomiting, and laxative abuse.

"At the time I was completely shocked," says a mother whose daughter died of an eating disorder some 15 years later. "How could someone as rich and famous as Karen Carpenter die at such a young age simply because she'd gone on a diet? Back then we really didn't understand the difference between just dieting and having an eating disorder. Her death made headlines all over the country, but they only said she'd died because her heart gave out, making us think that it was a biological or genetic problem. It wasn't until years later—when my own daughter was diagnosed—that I was finally able to learn more about how insidious eating disorders really are."

Although anorexia nervosa has been recognized as a medical condition for centuries, mental health professionals were just beginning to describe it in a coherent and consistent way at the time of Carpenter's death in 1983. Before the mid-1970s, psychiatric illnesses were characterized for the most part in very broad terms, like *neurosis*, that were based on concepts from psychoanalysis. Then in the 1970s, a profound revolution occurred in how psychiatric disorders were described and labeled. The profession shifted from characterizing disorders on the basis of the psychoanalytic theory of unconscious conflicts to categorizing behavioral and emotional problems on the basis of characteristics that are much easier to observe and describe. So the term *neurosis* was eliminated as an officially recognized diagnosis and was replaced by a large number of much more specific categories, including anorexia nervosa. This dramatic shift in how mental health professionals describe and name the illnesses they treat culminated in 1980 with the publication by the American Psychiatric Association of the *Diagnostic and Statistical Manual of Mental Disorders,* Third Edition, also referred to as *DSM-III*. The current version of this book, the *Diagnostic and Statistical Manual of Mental Disorders* (Fourth Edition, Text Revision, 2000) or *DSM-IV*, lists all of the officially recognized psychiatric disorders, including anorexia nervosa and bulimia nervosa, and is extremely important in influencing practitioners, researchers, and even insurance companies.

In developing *DSM-III* and *DSM-IV*, mental health practitioners were following the lead of the broader medical profession. Over several centuries, doctors have moved toward more and more specific definitions of illnesses, from describing a patient as having "fever" and "cough" to having "pneumococcal pneumonia." This transition has been useful for a variety of reasons, not the least of which is that it allows doctors to develop and provide much more specific and effective treatments. But a major difference still exists between the diagnosis of medical and psychiatric illnesses. The diagnosis of a psychiatric illness is based primarily on the patient's (and the family's) description of the problem, such as the occurrence of troublesome thoughts, behaviors, and feelings. In other areas of medicine, descriptions of symptoms, like complaints of pain, provide the first suggestions of the nature of the illness, but the final diagnosis is almost always confirmed by some other means, such as blood tests or sophisticated imaging procedures like MRIs or CAT scans. Such confirmatory diagnostic tests are not yet available for psychiatric illnesses, including anorexia nervosa, so doctors must arrive at a diagnosis by relying on the description of the patient's problem, their observations of the patient, and their own experience and judgment.

Some tests *can* reveal certain physical signs of eating disorders, such as low heart rate and blood pressure, dehydration, or electrolyte imbalances. But the key to making a diagnosis of anorexia nervosa involves keen observation and, to that end, parents can play a major role by watching for certain outward signs and symptoms, such as

- A dramatic weight loss not associated with a medical illness

- Self-deprecating remarks about being too fat despite noticeable weight loss

- A preoccupation with food, calories, and fat grams

- Restrictive eating habits that begin with the refusal to eat certain foods and progress to the elimination of whole categories of foods (e.g., fats, carbohydrates, etc.)

- Development of eating rituals (e.g., rearranging food on a plate to make it look like more has been eaten than actually has, cutting food into tiny bites, chewing food for an excessively long period, or eating foods in a certain order)

- Behavior indicating that weight loss, dieting, and control of food intake have become a primary concern

- Denial of hunger despite substantial loss of weight

- Wearing baggy clothes to hide extreme weight loss

- The avoidance of family meals and other social occasions that involve food

- The need to follow a rigid (usually excessive) exercise routine despite bad weather, injury, or illness

- Social isolation and withdrawal from family and friends

- Secretiveness, hostility, intolerance, and irritability

- Difficulty concentrating

- Weakness, faintness, or blackouts (in conjunction with other symptoms)

If you think your son or daughter is at risk for anorexia nervosa because he or she is exhibiting these signs, it is important to take them seriously and to act quickly to get your child help. These symptoms do not in themselves represent a formal diagnosis of the illness, but they are "red flags" that indicate your child needs to see a medical professional immediately. That professional will in turn assess your teen's symptoms in light of formal criteria or guidelines, likely to be those set forth in *DSM-IV.* These criteria are shown in Table 1 and are further discussed in the section called "What Does a *DSM* Diagnosis Mean?" (pp. 24–32).

Table 1
Diagnostic Criteria for Anorexia Nervosa

A. Refusal to maintain body weight at or above a minimally normal weight for age and height (e.g., weight loss leading to maintenance of body weight less than 85% of that expected; or failure to make expected weight gain during period of growth, leading to body weight less than 85% of that expected).
B. Intense fear of gaining weight or becoming fat, even though underweight.
C. Disturbance in the way in which one's body weight or shape is experienced, undue influence of body weight or shape on self-evaluation, or denial of the seriousness of the current low body weight.
D. In postmenarcheal females, amenorrhea, i.e., the absence of at least three consecutive menstrual cycles. (A woman is considered to have amenorrhea if her periods occur only following hormone, e.g., estrogen, administration.)

Specify type:
Restricting Type: during the current episode of anorexia nervosa, the person has not regularly engaged in binge-eating or purging behavior (i.e., self-induced vomiting or the misuse of laxatives, diuretics, or enemas)

Binge-Eating/Purging Type: during the current episode of anorexia nervosa, the person has regularly engaged in binge-eating or purging behavior (i.e., self-induced vomiting or the misuse of laxatives, diuretics, or enemas)

Source: Reprinted by permission from the *Diagnostic and statistical manual of mental disorders.* Copyright 2000. American Psychiatric Association.

Bulimia Nervosa

"Food was always a big part of Linda's life," Kay says of her daughter, who was diagnosed with bulimia nervosa. "Even when she was in kindergarten, she would take a box of cereal or crackers, go sit in front of the TV, and eat out of the box. She was also larger and more developed than most kids her age. As time went on, she became self-conscious about her size."

A month before Linda turned 12, she got the stomach flu, was out of school for a week, and lost ten pounds.

"When Linda returned to school," Kay says, "she got so much attention for losing weight that she decided to lose more. Eventually, she stopped eating anything but oranges. We kept trying to get her to eat, but nothing worked, and after four months, she'd lost 50 pounds. Then she suddenly started eating again. We were thrilled, but we were also amazed because she wasn't gaining any weight." She also began spending more and more time in the bathroom and, when Kay would go in to clean up, it appeared as if someone had vomited. Kay noticed changes in Linda's moods, too.

". . . after four months, she'd lost fifty pounds."

"Suddenly she wasn't our sweet little girl anymore. She started having trouble getting along with her sisters and grandmother, plus we also noticed lots of food disappearing. I would get home from the store and swear I had bought bagels, but the next morning when I went to look for them, they would be gone. I asked everybody in the house where they were and they all claimed they hadn't seen them. I started questioning whether the bagels had even made it home from the grocery store or if I had accidentally left them in the basket or on the counter."

According to Kay, Linda was also not the neatest person in the world and arguments ensued about her room always being a mess. An agreement was finally struck that if Linda wanted to leave it that way, she'd have to keep her bedroom door closed and would be responsible for putting away her clothes after they were laundered. After Linda left for camp the following summer, Kay went into Linda's room to give it a thorough cleaning.

"I found all these clothes that she'd purged in. They were shoved into drawers, under the bed, and stuffed in her soccer bag. There were enough clothes to fill a large lawn-size garbage bag. How there wasn't an incredible stench in that room is still beyond me. And a lot of the purging was dark matter, which I later found out from professionals was bile because that was how hard she was purging."

Linda exhibited classic symptoms of bulimia nervosa, a disease that was first clearly recognized as a disorder by the psychiatric community in 1979. It is characterized by episodes of binge eating large quantities of food during a short period of time, followed by purging (most commonly via self- or drug-induced vomiting, but laxatives and diuretics are also used), restricting food intake (via fasting or extreme dieting), or exercising excessively—all in an effort to avoid gaining weight from the binges. When vomiting is used, such binges can be repeated over several hours—the binger eats, vomits, and then eats again, with some patients reporting that they binge and purge up to 20 times during a 24-hour period.

While the binge-purge cycle of behavior is almost always done in secret and accompanied by feelings of self-disgust, shame, and being out of control, some claim they actually have no memory of binge eating and don't really taste the food they consume. Instead, the binge provides a sedative effect, almost as if the food they're eating acts like a tranquilizing drug that helps

. . . the binge-purge cycle of behavior is almost always done in secret . . .

them calm down and relieve stress. In such cases, it is only when the binge is over that the person experiences feelings of disgust and shame, which they may then try to assuage with the comforting effect of another binge.

The obsessive concern with shape and weight that characterizes anorexia nervosa is also a prominent feature of bulimia nervosa. The following story from Toni, now an adult recovering from bulimia nervosa, illustrates the extent to which such concerns drove her when she was a teen:

"I'd always been somewhat obsessed with how much I weighed, but never got to the point of starving myself because I loved food too much and couldn't give it up," Toni says. "I pretty much weighed the same thing my whole life, but had to work hard not to gain weight. Each day I'd decide what to eat and, if I had lunch, I either wouldn't eat dinner or, if I did, I'd eat something light, like a salad with no dressing or a small apple." One day, however, Toni forgot she'd been invited to a friend's house for dinner and went ahead and ate what she considered a "huge" lunch (in this case, a burger and fries). Upon returning home at the end of the day, she remembered the dinner invitation and became extremely distressed.

"I thought about what a good cook my friend's mom was and realized there would undoubtedly be lots of irresistible food I couldn't possibly pass up," Toni says. "Thinking I couldn't eat two big meals in one day, I suddenly got what I considered a brilliant idea: what goes in always comes out, so why not merely help it along?"

That was the day Toni decided to make herself vomit. She found it surprisingly easy to do and afterwards was absolutely euphoric because she felt cleansed and fresh and ready to partake of whatever delicious food her friend's mother might serve.

However, the evening became a blur because she kept thinking of herself as "gobbling up everything in sight."

"While I was eating, it was like I was in a trance and later imagined that it was probably a disgusting spectacle," she says. In hindsight, she now realizes that she really didn't eat much more than anyone else at the table. "Truth be told, I probably ate less than anyone there, but I still hated myself for 'pigging out' and, as soon as I returned home, I made myself throw up again."

Thus began a pattern of eating and then purging that would continue for years until Toni finally sought treatment at the behest of her boyfriend (later to become her husband). Yet to this day, she still has issues revolving around food and battles the urge to purge every time she eats more than she thinks she should.

"I still get a little panicked when I'm invited to a party, especially if the host or hostess tells me about all the great food they're going to serve. I guess that's the greatest irony of being bulimic. Because I've basically maintained the same weight over the years, no one ever suspects I have an eating disorder, so they continue to natter on about food without realizing how much it can torment me."

Toni's story also illustrates the point that, unlike those with anorexia nervosa—when self-starvation eventually gives them away physically, no matter how hard they try to hide it—people with bulimia nervosa stay close to or within their normal weight range and can appear perfectly healthy. As one parent says, "In most cases, you can't tell if someone has bulimia just by looking at them. You really have to listen to them and pay attention to their behavior." Indeed, bulimia nervosa is often so hard to spot that it can go undetected for years. The outward signs and symptoms that parents should watch for include the following:

". . . you can't tell if someone has bulimia just by looking at them."

- Evidence of purging behaviors (e.g., frequent trips to the bathroom after meals, signs of vomiting, discarded laxative or diuretic wrappers)
- Evidence of binge eating, including the disappearance of large amounts of food or the appearance of wrappers or empty containers indicating that a large amount of food has been consumed during a short period of time
- Swelling of the cheeks or around the jaw
- Calluses or scars on the back of the knuckles or hands from self-induced vomiting
- Dental problems, particularly the erosion of dental enamel from the backs of front teeth
- An excessive exercise regime despite bad weather, injury, or illness
- Behavior indicating that weight loss, dieting, and control of food intake have become primary concerns
- Mood swings

Again, these signs do not in themselves confirm a diagnosis of bulimia nervosa, but if your teen's behavior or outward appearance is raising such red flags, it is important that you consult a medical professional immediately about your child's condition, which too will likely be assessed according to the criteria of *DSM-IV.* The criteria for bulimia nervosa are shown in Table 2 and are further discussed in the section, "What Does a *DSM* Diagnosis Mean?" (see pp. 24–32).

Binge Eating Disorder

The two disorders we have just described, anorexia nervosa and bulimia nervosa, are the only two eating disorders formally rec-

Table 2
Diagnostic Criteria for Bulimia Nervosa

A. Recurrent episodes of binge eating. An episode of binge eating is characterized by both of the following:
   1. eating, in a discrete period of time (e.g., within any two-hour period), an amount of food that is definitely larger than most people would eat during a similar period of time and under similar circumstances
   2. a sense of lack of control over eating during the episode (e.g., a feeling that one cannot stop eating or control what or how much one is eating)
B. Recurrent inappropriate compensatory behavior in order to prevent weight gain, such as self-induced vomiting; misuse of laxatives, diuretics, enemas, or other medications; fasting; or excessive exercise.
C. The binge eating and inappropriate compensatory behaviors both occur, on average, at least twice a week for 3 months.
D. Self-evaluation is unduly influenced by body shape and weight.
E. The disturbance does not occur exclusively during episodes of anorexia nervosa.

Source: Reprinted by permission from the *Diagnostic and statistical manual of mental disorders.* Copyright 2000. American Psychiatric Association

ognized by *DSM-IV.* However, in recent years, there has been a great deal of interest in another disorder called "binge eating disorder." Because information about binge eating disorder was just emerging when *DSM-IV* was assembled, the criteria for this condition are only listed in an appendix of *DSM-IV* and are somewhat more controversial than those for the other two eating disorders. Nonetheless, the evidence that has emerged since the publication of *DSM-IV* in 2000 indicates that binge eating disorder is a serious condition that is associated with obesity and other major health complications. Like those with bulimia nervosa, binge eaters consume— rapidly and often secretly—large quantities

. . . binge eating disorder is a serious condition that is associated with obesity and other major health complications.

of food over a short period of time without regard to feelings of hunger or fullness. They also feel out of control during binges and then experience guilt, disgust, or shame following the binge. Yet unlike those with bulimia nervosa, they usually do not purge, dramatically restrict food intake, or exercise excessively to burn off the extra calories. For a diagnosis of binge eating disorder, according to the *DSM-IV* system, the binges must also be recurrent, taking place on an average of at least two days a week for six months or more. The diagnosis of binge eating disorder falls into the *DSM-IV* category of "eating disorders not otherwise specified," about which more will be said later in this chapter.

The National Institute of Diabetes and Digestive and Kidney Diseases (NIDDK) reported in 2001 that about 2% of all adults in the United States (as many as 4 million Americans) had binge eating disorder. The report also stated that the syndrome is somewhat more common among females than males, with three women for every two men being binge eaters. There is no solid information about how commonly binge eating disorder occurs among adolescents, but the dramatic increase in obesity among youngsters in recent years (discussed further in Chapter 5 of this book) raises concerns that a significant number of adolescents may be suffering from this disorder.

Eating Disorders in Males

Exact statistics as to how many males have eating disorders are elusive, but estimates have ranged from between 5% to 15% of all those diagnosed with anorexia nervosa and bulimia nervosa. However, an article published in the April 2001 issue of the *American Journal of Psychiatry* suggested the actual figure might be higher because males are less likely to seek treatment than females and their symptoms therefore go unreported, perhaps due to the misconception that eating disorders are solely "women's" diseases. Alternatively, because eating disorders are in fact more common among females, the symptoms of males who *do* seek treatment might initially be misdiagnosed, leading to a delay in receiving appropriate treatment. This is what happened in the case of Cathleen's son Phil.

"Phil had digestive problems for a few months and kept losing a lot of weight while seeing different doctors who were trying to figure out what was wrong," she says. "His tests were positive in the sense that something was indeed awry with his system, but they just couldn't pinpoint it. With each doctor, I continually shared my concerns that his problem might be emotional rather than physical. I explained our home situation [Cathleen and Phil's father had separated], Phil's drive to be 'perfect,' how he always seemed to be stressed out, and other things I'd noticed." But the doctors all thought Phil's problem was primarily physical and he was eventually diagnosed as having celiac disease (also known as gluten intolerance).

"Being a boy may have been the reason the doctors overlooked the possibility of his having an eating disorder," Cathleen adds, "but I think the fact that his digestive system was a mess and the fact that his tests were positive were what threw them off."

Cathleen finally insisted on taking Phil to a clinic that specialized in eating disorders, and it was only then that the diagnosis of anorexia nervosa was made. The doctor there even praised Cathleen for seeking another opinion about Phil.

"Being a boy may have been the reason the doctors overlooked the possibility of his having an eating disorder . . ."

"The doctor told me that not many parents would come forward to ask for psychological help for their children when they'd already been told that the problem was physical," she states.

It also may have been more difficult to think that Phil had an eating disorder because his thinness seemed simply to reflect his participation in certain activities. Phil was on the high school track team. Athletes, as well as dancers, actors, and models, must constantly focus on their fitness and appearance, and in sports like cross-country, track, and swimming, slimmer bodies are the norm. It would be easy for parents to mistake their son's obsession with weight loss as merely a byproduct of his activities rather than as a manifestation of an eating disorder.

So what might indicate that your son has an eating disorder? The red flags mentioned previously are no different and no less serious for boys than they are for girls. Watch for

- An abnormally low weight or significant fluctuations in weight not due to medical illness.
- Purging behaviors intended to induce weight loss. (One study in 1998 found that 4% of sixth- to eighth-grade boys reported self-induced vomiting or and laxative use to lose weight.)
- Persistent intense concerns with weight or shape.
- Persistent attempts to diet or lose weight despite being at a normal or low weight.
- Social withdrawal and isolation from activities involving food and/or eating.

What Does a *DSM* Diagnosis Mean?

As we have already mentioned, *DSM-IV* provides the set of guidelines most widely used by mental health professionals to describe the exact nature of a patient's problem and to assign a diagnosis. Once an accurate diagnosis has been made, it is easier to know what treatments are appropriate and likely to be successful. This is clearly true for purely physical conditions: Bacterial pneumonia responds to antibiotics while viral pneumonia does not. And it is no less true of psychiatric disorders, but with mental illnesses like eating disorders, nailing down the correct diagnosis can be a challenge. The *DSM-IV* diagnostic criteria for eating disorders are based on signs and symptoms reported by patients seeking treatment because of distress over their symptoms or because of medical, psychological, or social impairment resulting from these problems. Eating disorders professionals accept, for the most part, the *DSM-IV* criteria for the two main syndromes of anorexia nervosa and bulimia nervosa, but they recognize at least one major problem with them: The criteria are so strict that the majority of patients treated in clinical settings don't actually meet the full definition of either of these two syndromes. They are instead grouped into the loosely termed and poorly characterized "eating disorder not otherwise specified" (EDNOS) category.

Even the criteria for the two main syndromes themselves are sometimes subject to debate, with some in the mental health field arguing that the guidelines are less than perfect in accurately defining the diagnostic complexities of either illness. As shown in Table 1, the first criterion for anorexia nervosa—Criterion A—deals with weight loss. While this would not seem to be a controversial concept, clinicians do not unanimously agree about how weight loss for those with anorexia nervosa should be calculated, especially in adolescents. Some investigators emphasize the amount lost from an original baseline (i.e., the individual's weight before the problem started), and others emphasize weight loss below a normal weight for age and height.

. . . in anorexia nervosa, dieting behavior often has an obsessive quality that is difficult for patients to "control."

The term *refusal* in Criterion A is also problematic, as it implies a voluntary and explicit decision not to eat. But in anorexia nervosa, dieting behavior often has an obsessive quality that is difficult for patients to "control." In other words, their "refusal" seems more driven than explicitly chosen.

Regarding the second criterion—Criterion B—it's true that many individuals with anorexia nervosa do acknowledge an intense fear of gaining weight or becoming fat. But it is also true that younger individuals, as well as those who are not motivated to seek treatment, sometimes firmly deny they fear gaining weight, despite behavior that strongly suggests otherwise. The criterion focuses on a psychological factor—the emotion of fear—which can be difficult to be sure of when the patient adamantly denies it.

The third criterion—Criterion C—is perhaps the least debated in the field but it is especially complex, as it attempts to define the core psychological features of anorexia nervosa. A distorted image about body weight or shape can be indicated by the individual's statements about feeling fat or about specific parts of the body being too large, even when that person is emaciated. Moreover, individuals with anorexia nervosa are remarkably successful at remaining underweight, appearing to derive a feeling of accomplishment by evaluating themselves in terms of their thinness. To admit the seriousness of low body weight would be to acknowledge the need to gain weight, which is a terrifying notion to those with this illness.

Of the *DSM* criteria for anorexia nervosa, the last—amenorrhea, or the loss of menstrual periods—is particularly controversial among researchers. The amenorrhea occurs because of a decrease in the release of hormones by a part of the brain called the hypothalamus. This change triggers a "chain reaction" of decreases in the release of hormones from the pituitary gland and from the ovaries. The insufficient amount of estrogen coming from the ovaries results in the amenorrhea. In the last few years, it has been learned that, in anorexia nervosa, the hypothalamus reduces the secretion of hormones because the amount of leptin, a hormone released into the blood by fat cells, is too low. In other words, in order for adolescent girls to have normal menstrual cycles, their bodies have to have a normal amount of fat tissue. If there is too little fat tissue, as in anorexia nervosa, normal menstruation stops.

So, what's the problem with *DSM-IV*'s requiring amenorrhea for the diagnosis of anorexia nervosa? The difficulty lies in the fact that several investigators have described patients who meet all diagnostic criteria for anorexia nervosa except amenorrhea and have found that, aside from this exception, these patients appear no different from those individuals who do meet all the criteria. Presumably, these young women still have just enough body fat to allow their hormone systems to function. These observations, in addition to the occasional difficulty of obtaining an accurate history of menstrual patterns from patients, suggest that amenorrhea may not be such a useful criterion for anorexia nervosa.

To further complicate diagnosis, *DSM-IV* also suggests that individuals with anorexia nervosa be described as belonging to one of two mutually exclusive subtypes: those who do not binge or purge during an episode of anorexia nervosa (the restricting type, or AN-R) and those who do (the binge eating/purging type, or AN-B/P). These subtypes were included in the *DSM-IV* criteria for anorexia nervosa because of evidence of other health and mental health problems in AN-B/P patients: Their binge eating and purging behaviors predispose them to medical problems less frequently associated with the restricting type, and they have a higher frequency of impulsive behaviors, such as suicide attempts, self-mutilation, stealing, and alcohol or substance abuse, than do AN-R patients.

As for bulimia nervosa, the *DSM-IV*'s diagnostic criteria for this disorder can be equally challenging to interpret. As shown in Table 2, Criterion A defines a binge eating episode as characterized by amount ("larger than most people would eat"), duration ("in a discrete period of time"), and psychological state ("a sense of lack of control"). The relative importance of these elements and the definitions offered are open to interpretation, however. For example, many patients state that they are binge eating when they eat amounts of food that are no larger than most people eat, and they believe that the sense of loss of control is more important than the amount ingested. Thus, unless they *also* binge regularly on large amounts of food, they should not be given the diagnosis of bulimia nervosa, according to *DSM-IV*.

Criterion B, which describes recurrent and inappropriate compensatory behaviors, includes both those that are easily characterized (self-induced vomiting) and those that are not: What, for example, constitutes "misuse" of laxatives and diuretics, and what defines "excessive exercise"? Criterion C requires that the binge eating and inappropriate compensatory behaviors occur on average at least twice a week for three months, but studies suggest that individuals with somewhat lower frequencies of binge eating closely resemble those who meet Criterion C. And Criterion D, which states that the individual's self-evaluation is unduly influenced by body shape and weight, is part of the anorexia nervosa criterion as well and attempts to capture an important psychological dimension of the disorder.

. . . what defines "excessive exercise"?

But the line between "undue influence" and the overconcern with body shape and weight that is often seen especially in adolescent girls is uncertain.

Given the limitations and the interpretative challenges of the *DSM-IV* criteria for anorexia nervosa and bulimia nervosa, many people whose symptoms fail to meet these criteria end up being grouped into the EDNOS category. Including binge eating disorder and all other disorders of eating, which in turn are inadequately described, it is sometimes called the "EDNOS grab bag" as a result. This means, for example, that a severely underweight 16-year-old girl who, describing herself as fat, refuses to eat anything except celery but who has not stopped menstruating for three consecutive months would not be diagnosed as having anorexia nervosa because she failed to meet the *DSM-IV*'s Criterion D for amenorrhea. She'd fall into the EDNOS category instead. So would a teenager who binges and purges only once a week, rather than the twice-a-week requirement dictated by Criterion C for a diagnosis of bulimia nervosa. And so would individuals with other serious eating disturbances outside the *DSM-IV*'s criteria for the two major syndromes. They all belong to a large group of people with the same vague EDNOS diagnosis. In fact, according to data collected on over 700 people with eating disorders from five clinical centers around the country, 49% to 71% did not meet the full *DSM* criteria for anorexia nervosa or bulimia nervosa but received the EDNOS diagnosis instead, as did over 50% of the adolescents in this group.

The *DSM-IV* criteria for anorexia nervosa and bulimia nervosa are useful in helping the medical community to recognize and describe people with severe disturbances of eating behavior. But clearly, the *DSM-IV* system fails to provide useful categories for a substantial number of individuals with significant eating disorder symptoms. A possible alternative to the *DSM-IV* categories for adolescents is the American Academy of Pediatrics' *Diagnostic and Statistical Manual for Primary Care, Child and Adolescent Version* (1996), a classification system developed to help primary care providers to better recognize and diagnose child and adolescent mental health conditions, including normal variations and problems as well as disorders. Its classification scheme for eating disorders—in which "variations" represent minor symptoms related to eating or body image, and "problems" reflect more serious disturbances—is broader than the *DSM*'s, and it includes a hierarchy of clinical presentations (e.g., of binge eating, dieting, and body image problems) that do not reach full *DSM-IV* diagnostic criteria. This system may help to define a wide range of potentially important eating problems among adolescents, but its actual usefulness has received little experimental examination to date. It is not known, for example, how often, or whether, its variations or problems advance to full *DSM-IV* syndromes.

Another set of criteria established to describe the wide range of eating problems seen among children is that of the Great Ormond Street Hospital in London. These criteria use determined weight loss, abnormal perception about weight and/or body shape, and morbid preoccupation with weight and/or shape for the diagnosis of anorexia nervosa. The bulimia nervosa criteria include recurrent binges and purges, sense of lack of control, and morbid preoccupation with shape and weight. Specific criteria for other disorders are also included, such as "food avoidance emotional disorder," a condition characterized by depression or other emotional problems that affect the child's appetite and result in the avoidance of food, and "selective eating," a disorder in which the child will eat only a very narrow range of "safe" or "acceptable" foods and may become extremely upset if encouraged or forced to eat foods beyond this range. While promising in their attempt to broaden diagnostic categories, the Great Ormond Street criteria have not yet been widely used, either by practitioners or by researchers. What does this bewildering array of criteria mean to you as a parent faced with a child who may have an eating disorder? They mean that defining the boundaries between minor variations of normal adolescent eating and the more serious eating disorders is still something of a complex challenge even for the professionals. Arriving at an accurate and helpful diagnosis may not be an easy or straightforward task. Much still remains to be learned about these illnesses in order to refine the criteria by which they are best diagnosed by the medical profession. For now, with all its imperfections, the DSM-IV system remains the standard by which your own child's mental health status will be assessed and according to which decisions about treatment and health care coverage will be made.

> . . . defining the boundaries between minor variations of normal adolescent eating and the more serious eating disorders is still something of a complex challenge . . .

As the person who knows your child best, you can help to ensure that these diagnostic standards are applied appropriately by, first and foremost, providing the best information you can to your child's doctor about the signs and symptoms—the red flags—you've seen that led you to worry he or she may have an eating disorder. When meeting the doctor for the first time, for example, come prepared to answer questions about when these signs began, how often they occur, how long they last, and how severe they seem. Others in your child's daily life—teachers, athletic coaches, school counselors, for example—may be able to help you in this regard, by offering their own observations of your child's behavior in class or the school cafeteria or the playing field. Chances are they've seen at least some of the same signs in school that you have at home. Ask them, and together you can gather the kind of information that will help the doctor understand your child's symptoms well enough to arrive at an accurate diagnosis.

Before a diagnosis is made, a complete medical checkup will likely be recommended to rule out other diseases that could be causing symptoms similar to an eating disorder. Among the general medical conditions that may cause such symptoms are intestinal problems like inflammatory bowel disease and celiac disease (the initial diagnosis Cathleen's son Phil received), diabetes, hyperthyroidism (overactive thyroid), neurological conditions, including brain tumors, and chronic diseases or infections. Psychiatric disorders such as serious depression or obsessive-compulsive disorder (OCD) may also be present. These and other psychiatric conditions are discussed later in this chapter, in the section "What Other Conditions Can Co-exist with Eating Disorders?

How Common Are Eating Disorders in Adolescents?

Although the symptoms of eating disorders are known to originate primarily in adolescence, research on their frequency (prevalence) among adolescents is surprisingly limited. Most studies have focused principally on the occurrence of these disorders in adults, but even for this age group, knowledge is limited with regard to how many individuals actually have an eating disorder and who in particular is vulnerable to developing a specific type, such as anorexia nervosa or bulimia nervosa. As mentioned in Chapter 1, however, experts do seem to agree on these statistics: that eating disorders occur in approximately 1% (anorexia nervosa) to 3% (bulimia nervosa) of women

. . . eating disorders occur in approximately 1% (anorexia nervosa) to 3% (bulimia nervosa) of women . . .

during their lives, and prevalence rates among men are approximately one-tenth of those observed in women.

The relatively few studies that have focused on the prevalence of eating disorders in adolescents vary considerably in their approach—in the number and gender of the individuals studied, in their location (ranging from teens in a single New York City school to those in an entire county of New Jersey to those in a nationwide sample in Great Britain), in the methods used to screen and identify individuals who may have an eating disorder, and in the ways in which these studies report their findings. For example, the nationwide study in Great Britain surveyed over 10,000 girls and boys between the ages of 5 and 15, but did not report detailed information about the specific types of eating disorders that had been identified (anorexia nervosa or bulimia nervosa) or the gender of those affected with them. Moreover, the ethnic diversity of the individuals in this and most other studies was not explored.

The variability in these studies, along with the relative lack of research conducted on this age group overall, makes it difficult to say confidently how many adolescents in fact experience an eating disorder. The figures cited in Chapter 1 from the American Academy of Pediatrics (0.5% of teenage girls have anorexia nervosa, 1% to 5% have bulimia nervosa, with up to 10% of all cases of eating disorders occurring in males) are therefore only rough estimates. Moreover, some experts have expressed concern that such prevalence figures may seriously underestimate the magnitude of the problem among adolescents because they focus primarily on those teens who meet the full *DSM* criteria for a diagnosis of anorexia nervosa or bulimia nervosa. What about those adolescents who show the core features of these disorders but whose symptoms do not meet the *DSM*'s required severity or duration? Because these symptoms may represent the first signs of the development of a full-syndrome disorder, a look at their prevalence gives some indication of the size of the "at risk" group.

In 1990, the Centers for Disease Control and Prevention developed the Youth Risk Behavior Surveillance System to monitor health risk behaviors that contribute markedly to the leading causes of death, disability, and social problems among youth and young adults in the United States. The system conducts school-based Youth Risk Behavior Surveys (YRBS) of ninth- through twelfth-grade students every two years. The students respond to these surveys anonymously; among the questions are several about current attempts to lose weight, weight loss, or weight maintenance efforts, such as vomiting, diet pills, and "other methods."

Consistently, the YRBS has found that about two of every three female students report trying to lose weight, compared to one in four male students. Trying to gain weight is quite common among boys (about 40%), whereas only a minority of girls (about 8%) try to be heavier. The YRBS for 1999 and 2001 also suggest that inappropriate efforts to lose weight or to keep from gaining weight—what in *DSM-IV* are considered "inappropriate compensatory behaviors"—appear to be disturbingly common, especially among girls. In 1999, for example, over 18% of girls fasted as compared to over 6% of boys who did so; nearly 11% of girls used diet pills, whereas only about

4% of boys did; and over 7% of girls resorted to vomiting or laxative abuse, as compared to about 2% of boys. The YRBS also examines ethnic group differences in the prevalence of weight-related behaviors. In 2001, white and Hispanic girls were found to be significantly more likely than black girls to report inappropriate compensatory behaviors. Almost one in four (23.1%) Hispanic students and one in five white students (19.7%), compared to 15% of black students, reported that she had gone without eating for 24 or more hours to control her weight. Vomiting, or laxative use, for weight-control reasons was reported by over 10%, 8%, and 4% of Hispanic, white, and black girls, respectively. How many girls in this sample would meet diagnostic criteria for an eating disorder is unknown, because the YRBS does not include questions covering the complete set of diagnostic criteria for anorexia nervosa and bulimia nervosa. Nevertheless, it does show that a considerable number of female students practices potentially health-damaging behaviors, such as vomiting—in short, cause for real concern.

While the YRBS did not assess binge eating, one 2003 study of boys and girls in public schools provides information about binge eating in adolescents. Binge eating was considered present if the child answered yes to a question about overeating with loss of control, at least a few times a week, and about feeling upset "some" or "a lot" by overeating. More girls (3.1%) than boys (0.9%) met criteria for binge eating, and the results suggested that binge eating was significantly correlated with weight (actually, with the body mass index, or BMI, a measure of weight relative to height) in girls and boys. Binge eating was only slightly more common in white girls (2.6%) than black girls (1.6%) or Hispanic girls (1.7%), and was reported by a surprisingly large number of Asian American girls (5.9%). Therefore, binge eating appears to be disturbingly common and to occur among ethnically diverse groups.

What Causes Eating Disorders and Who Is at Risk?

Despite extensive information about the characteristics of eating disorders, solid knowledge of their actual causes has so far eluded the scientific community. Simply put, no one can tell you, with any scientific certainty, why your child has developed an eating disorder. Still, because of the obvious importance of the question, investigators are urgently committed to uncover information about these disorders that could shed light on their causes and ultimately improve their treatment and prevention. In this section, we'll first explain why identifying the causes of eating disorders is so challenging, and then focus on several factors that may contribute to the risk of developing an eating disorder.

. . . no one can tell you, with any scientific certainty, why your child has developed an eating disorder.

If there was a simple, straightforward, and single cause for eating disorders, how would we recognize it? We'd expect that it would be found in all people who developed an eating disorder, that the cause would be present *before* the disorder began, and that the cause would not be found among people without the illness. An example of a simple relationship between a cause and an illness is AIDS. A virus, called HIV, causes AIDS: AIDS only develops among people who have contracted HIV, and people who do not have HIV do not develop AIDS. The causes of psychiatric illnesses, including eating disorders, are much more complicated. It does not appear that eating disorders have a single cause; rather, multiple influences, called "risk factors," seem to combine and interact to eventually result in the occurrence of anorexia nervosa or bulimia nervosa. As we will discuss, some of these risk factors appear to be an individual's personal characteristics, like his or her sex, and others appear to be in the world around the individual, like the culture in which he or she grows up. Because so many factors seem possibly to have an influence, it has been very difficult for researchers to sort out which ones are most significant.

Part of the problem in identifying the important risk factors is that eating disorders, especially full-blown anorexia nervosa and bulimia nervosa, are not very common. As we described in the last section, only a few percent of young women will ever develop an eating disorder that meets *DSM-IV* criteria. This poses a real challenge for researchers. If eating disorders are caused by the interaction of multiple "causes," each of which increases the chances by a small amount, a study to prove these risk factors were really important would have to follow thousands of young people for many years, from before the eating disorders developed until early adulthood, when all the people who were going to develop an eating disorder would have been identified. The scientific and financial requirements for such a study are daunting, and to date, no large study of this type has been done.

What researchers have identified are *possible* risk factors— biological, environmental, social, and psychological phenomena that appear to increase the likelihood that an adolescent will develop either eating-disorder symptoms or a full-blown syndrome. A large number of such risk factors has been described, but the scientific evidence supporting many of them is far from overwhelming. In the next section, we will describe several risk factors about which some information is available, and which may help you to think through why your child might be more likely to have a problem.

Gender

Being female is the most obvious and "reliable" risk factor for the development of an eating disorder. Many theories ranging from the sociocultural to the biological have been offered for this phenomenon, but no conclusive explanation has yet been found as to why, consistently across various cultures, more females than males have these disorders.

Puberty

Although the onset of eating disorders can occur at any time throughout the life span, the greatest risk period for onset, especially of anorexia nervosa, is around the time of and just following puberty. Disturbances in eating and weight-related behavior have also been found to be clearly present in preadolescent girls. As is true with gender, there is no real certainty about why the onset of puberty increases risk, but again, theories ranging from the sociocultural (girls may be more vulnerable during puberty to social pressures to be thin, particularly in the context of their bodily changes, such as increases in fat stores) to the biological (hormonal changes that can trigger other biological processes) have been suggested.

. . . the greatest risk period for onset, especially of anorexia nervosa, is around the time of puberty.

Brain Chemistry

Evidence suggests that women with eating disorders have some disturbance in the brain's serotonin system. One of several neurotransmitters, or chemicals that act as messengers in the brain, serotonin is involved in the regulation of many normal phenomena, including both mood and behavior, such as eating. But while there is good circumstantial evidence that the serotonin system of individuals with eating disorders is not entirely normal, exactly what is wrong with it is not clear. Furthermore, it is very difficult to sort out the "cart or horse" issue: Do serotonergic abnormalities precede the development of the eating disorder and increase the risk? Or are the abnormalities only another of the many physical changes that result from disturbances in weight and eating behavior? A recent, provocative finding identified serotonin abnormalities in people who had anorexia nervosa but who are now entirely recovered, leading researchers to speculate that the abnormalities might have been present *before* the illness began and have somehow increased the chances of its occurrence.

Genetics

Studies have demonstrated that relatives of those with eating disorders have a greater lifetime prevalence of having the disorders themselves. Relatives of individuals with anorexia nervosa and bulimia nervosa also have significantly increased rates of eating disorders that do not meet full diagnostic criteria, suggesting a broad spectrum of eating-related pathology in families. Thus, there is good evidence that eating disorders tend to run in families. In addition, studies of twins suggest that genes are a significant contributor to the familial occurrence of eating disorders. That is, if an eating disorder develops in one twin, it is much more likely that the other twin will also develop

> . . . there is good evidence that eating disorders tend to run in families.

it if the twins are identical (i.e., they have an identical genetic makeup) than if they are not identical (fraternal).

But despite the compelling evidence that genetic influences contribute to an individual's vulnerability to develop an eating disorder, no single gene or set of genes has consistently emerged as strongly associated with either anorexia nervosa or bulimia nervosa. It seems likely that the development of these disorders is influenced not just by an individual's genetic makeup or just by that individual's personal and social environment but also by a complex interaction between the two dimensions. The same may hold true for other behaviors or disorders that have been found to have a hereditary component, such as binge eating, obesity, and obsessive-compulsiveness, itself a possible coexisting condition in eating-disordered individuals.

Sociocultural Factors: The "Thin Ideal" and the Role of the Media

The emphasis on thinness—and more generally, on an individual's weight and body shape as measures of personal worth—does seem pervasive in our society, and indeed weight concerns and dieting are the norm in the United States and other developed countries. Does this cultural phenomenon necessarily predispose one to acquiring an eating disorder? Of all the possible risk factors to be implicated in the onset of these disorders, this one—the predominantly Western cultural ideal of thinness—may be the most familiar to the public because of the persistent presentation of images of thin, attractive, and successful young people in the mass media. Donna, whose daughter Chelsey was diagnosed with anorexia nervosa at age 16, has much to say on this very point:

"Our culture equates success and beauty and popularity with a thin body. Because those skin-and-bones actresses, models, and singers are highly successful, they also become role models for our children. For heaven's sake, they're *stars* and every magazine you pick up has one of them on the cover. Then, inside the magazine, there are tons of ads about dieting and losing weight. On TV it's the same thing

"Our culture equates success and beauty and popularity with a thin body. . . ."

and even when you go on the Internet, you get pop-up ads claiming if you just buy a certain diet book or diet pill, you too can be as thin and happy as that movie star. It's appalling that positive things are attributed to having a thin body. But how can we expect our children to see themselves for who and what they are when they are continually bombarded with all these images?"

The fact that eating disorders are described primarily in developed countries does suggest that media-driven Western cultural influences, particularly the thin ideal, are somehow involved in their onset, but precisely how this may be so remains unclear. In industrialized countries, where exposure to the thin ideal and dieting are nearly universal, where dissatisfaction with the size and shape of one's own body is chronic especially in women, and where the overwhelming majority of women say they would like to lose weight, only a very small number of young women actually develops clinically significant eating disorders. Moreover, the incidence of eating disorders elsewhere in the world suggests that the illnesses are not confined to areas that embrace the Western ideal of slimness. While the Western cultural imperative to be thin in order to be attractive may, indeed, increase the chances that one will develop an eating disorder, other factors must certainly also be important.

Race and Socioeconomic Status

Traditionally, eating disorders, and particularly anorexia nervosa, were thought to affect only the white upper middle class. One study in 1995 did find that the parents of children with anorexia nervosa had a greater number of years of education (reflecting greater economic means), but in general, eating disorders can occur across all races and cultures, regardless of economic status.

Personality Traits

Anorexia nervosa has been consistently linked to such personality and temperamental traits as negative self-evaluation, low self-esteem, extreme compliance (submission to the wishes or suggestions of others), obsessiveness, and perfectionism. These traits continue to characterize individuals with anorexia nervosa even after recovery. In fact, some studies have focused only on recovered individuals and have presumed that traits persisting after recovery represent enduring traits that preceded the onset of the disorder. The potential weakness of this presumption is

---

Eating Disorders Don't Discriminate

One of the biggest misconceptions about the prevalence of eating disorders is that they affect only "white girls." However, as the Office on Women's Health (OWH) points out, an increasing number of girls and boys from all ethnic and racial groups are suffering from eating disorders, although their cases can go unreported "due to the lack of studies that include representatives from these groups." As Drs. Marian Fitzgibbon and Melinda Stolley speculate in *Minority Women: The Untold Story*, the reason for the exclusion of minorities in early research on eating disorders was due to most studies only being conducted on college campuses or in hospital clinics. They state, "For reasons related to economics, access to care, and cultural attitudes toward psychological treatment, middle-class white females were the ones seeking treatment and thus became the subjects of research." Also, the OWH surmises that girls of different ethnic and cultural groups may not seek treatment because of "difficulty in locating culturally sensitive treatment centers."

that these traits may not have existed prior to the development of the disease and instead could represent personality or trait "scars" from having had the disease.

Dieting

Dieting is one of the most talked-about possible risk factors for eating disorders, and yet one of the least well characterized. Part of the problem is with terminology. The term *dieting* itself is complex, laden with many meanings, and is used to refer to a variety of attitudes and behaviors. At its most basic, the word *diet* means simply "habitual nutrition"—that is, what we ordinarily eat and drink in order to live day to day. A "special diet" might be one in which certain foods are off limits—say, because they cause an allergic reaction, or because they raise cholesterol, or because they're prohibited by one's religion. And then there's the type of diet one goes on in order to gain or, more often, to lose weight.

It is, of course, in the sense of losing weight that most people use the term. The National Task Force on the Prevention and Treatment of Obesity defines dieting as "the intentional and sustained restriction of caloric intake for the purposes of reducing body weight or changing body shape, resulting in a significant negative energy balance." This implies that, strictly speaking, dieting should only be called "dieting" if it is associated with weight loss. From this perspective, attempts to restrict caloric intake that do not result in weight loss represent unsuccessful dieting, and it is important to note that such attempts are frequently described by individuals with symptoms of eating disorders. Unfortunately, though, the literature on eating disorders does not distinguish between successful and unsuccessful attempts to restrict caloric intake, making it difficult to determine whether successful and unsuccessful dieting play similar roles in the development of eating disorders.

Other terms complicate the literature as well. *Restrained eating* and *dietary restraint,* for example, are frequently used in discussions of risk factors for the development and maintenance of eating disorders. Dietary restraint, a frame of mind linked with the attempt to diet, tends to be associated with unsuccessful dieting, but both it and *restrained eating* are used to describe a range of attitudes and behaviors, including food avoidance.

In part because of these terminological issues, the research on the relationship between dieting and eating disorders is inconclusive and does not resolve the degree to which the "dieting" commonly engaged in by large numbers of young women should be considered a risk factor for eating disorders. What may be a clearer distinction, however, is the difference between dieting and *unhealthy weight-loss behaviors*—that is, activities that are associated with some risk of physical harm, such as self-induced vomiting, laxative and diet pill abuse, complete food avoidance for extended periods of time (fasting), and excessive exercise to lose weight. These types of behavior *are* relevant in discussions of risk factors for eating disorders, as a considerable number of young people engages in these practices, and it is likely that these behaviors are, for many individuals, the beginning of the development of an eating disorder meeting full *DSM-IV* criteria.

. . . the research on the relationship between dieting and eating disorders is inconclusive . . .

Activities with a Focus on Body Shape and Weight

Activities that emphasize weight and appearance (e.g., ballet, gymnastics) have been investigated as independent risk factors for the development of anorexia nervosa. Ballet dancers in particular have been found to have an increased prevalence of both diagnosable eating disorders and disordered eating symptoms, with a prevalence of *DSM-IV* anorexia nervosa that is 4 to 25 times higher than in the general population. Models, actresses, entertainers, and others whose appearance plays a major role in their careers are also likely to be at a higher risk for developing an eating disorder. But even here, cause and effect are hard to separate, as it may be that the athletic and artistic worlds attract individuals who are already preoccupied with shape and weight or had other risk factors that contribute both to their choice of a career and to the emergence of an eating disorder.

Models, actresses, entertainers, and others whose appearance plays a major role in their careers are also likely to be at a higher risk for developing an eating disorder.

Family Relationships

In the 1950s, when the occurrence of virtually all emotional problems was explained on the basis of theories from psychoanalysis, it was widely believed that particular patterns of family interaction, especially early in life, were causative factors in the development of eating disorders. These ideas were never confirmed scientifically, and investigators are currently much more cautious about ascribing the risk of eating disorders to the family environment. There is often dysfunction in the family when a child has anorexia nervosa or bulimia nervosa. But it is very hard to know whether such family problems have any role in the development of the disorder or whether they are simply manifestations of distress about an ill child in an otherwise normally functioning family.

Peer Influence

Given the adolescent vulnerability to peer pressure, some teens may adopt the excessive concern with body shape, weight, dieting, or binge eating that they observe in their friends, but how much this "contagion" effect plays a role in eating disturbances has received little study to date. (Further attention to peer influence or support in the maintenance of eating disorders is given in Chapter 5, particularly in the discussion of the "Pro-Ana" and "Pro-Mia" Web sites, pp. 155–156.)

Childhood Trauma

Much has been written in the popular media about the role of childhood trauma, and particularly sexual abuse, in the development of eating disorders. Although there are significant limitations on our knowledge, research studies have found that individuals with eating disorders are more likely to have histories of such traumatic experiences than those without the disorders. However, there are two additional important findings. First, among individuals with anorexia nervosa and bulimia nervosa, only a minority appear to have such histories. By no means can one conclude that because a young woman has developed an eating disorder, she must have been abused as a child. Second, the occurrence of childhood trauma increases one's chances of developing *many* emotional and behavioral problems, so such trauma is probably best viewed as a nonspecific risk factor for a range of problems later in life.

What Other Conditions Can Coexist with Eating Disorders?

It is an unfortunate but highly common occurrence that many adolescents with eating disorders struggle with other emotional, behavioral, and psychological problems as well. In fact, across all age groups, over 70% of those with anorexia nervosa and about 75% of those with bulimia nervosa are affected by them. Whether these problems—called "comorbidities" by health professionals—are possible causes or consequences of the eating disorder can be difficult to determine, but what is clear is that their existence can complicate or delay the diagnosis and treatment of the eating disorder. Valerie illustrates this point with the following story:

"At 13 or 14 years of age, our daughter suddenly showed very little interest in her personal appearance. She started wearing baggy clothes, spent large amounts of time in her room by herself with the door closed, and had no interest in doing those activities with family and friends that had always been important to her. She wasn't sleeping well either. We didn't know what was wrong. We feared she was involved with drugs. That was not the case. This was actually the first sign of depression. We recently found out that chronic depression and anorexia go hand-in-hand for many patients.

"Our daughter had dual problems that took years to diagnose. We did not have any prior knowledge of eating disorders. After we knew she was anorexic, we still faced a medical community that had no idea what to do for her. She was in and out of facilities for years before we found out what was wrong with her. She had been misdiagnosed many times. No one seemed to know how to treat her. Because of suicide attempts and irrational behavior, she was committed to a state mental hospital, where she was tube-fed but received no treatment for her anorexia except nutritional supplements. After two-plus years, she was released and told she needed to be treated by someone who specialized in anorexia. To us, it came as no surprise because, by that time, we felt like we knew more than the doctors."

. . . other emotional, behavioral, and psychological disorders often share symptoms similar to those of eating disorders . . .

Valerie's frustration with the difficulties in recognizing and treating her daughter's coexisting illnesses is understandable. Unfortunately, other emotional, behavioral, and psychological disorders often share symptoms similar to those of eating disorders, which can often make diagnosis difficult.

Other disorders that commonly occur with eating disorders are the following:

- Mood disorders. Significant mood disturbances, termed "affective disorders" by mental health professionals, commonly co-occur with anorexia nervosa and bulimia nervosa. In particular, many individuals with eating disorders also suffer from major depressive disorder. According to the *DSM-IV,* major depression essentially involves either being depressed or irritable nearly all the time or losing interest or enjoyment in almost everything. It is not just a passing case of the blues, nor is it a sign of personal weakness, nor can it simply be wished away. It lasts for at least two weeks and is associated with other symptoms, such as a change in eating or sleeping habits, lack of energy, feelings of worthlessness, trouble with concentration, or thoughts of suicide. Affective disorders like major depression may begin before or after the onset of eating disorders, or the disorders can begin at the same time.

- Anxiety disorders. People with anxiety disorders suffer from exaggerated worry and tension, even when there is little to worry about. Symptoms can manifest themselves physically as well as emotionally. Two types of anxiety disorders that most frequently predate the onset of anorexia nervosa or bulimia nervosa are social phobia (excessive self-consciousness in social situations) and obsessive-compulsive disorder or OCD (becoming obsessed with a certain idea and/or feeling compelled by an urgent need to engage in certain rituals).

- Substance use disorders. Individuals with eating disorders, especially those with bulimia nervosa and those with the binge-purge subtype of anorexia nervosa, have some tendency to engage in substance use behavior, such as the abuse of alcohol, cocaine, and marijuana. In both anorexia nervosa and bulimia nervosa, substance abuse tends to begin after the onset of the illness.

- Personality disorders. Defined as a constellation of personality traits that significantly impair one's ability to function socially or cause personal distress, personality disorders are considered by some researchers to be a significant comorbidity with eating disorders. Among the personality disorders that may occur with anorexia nervosa, for example, is avoidant personality disorder, which is characterized by hypersensitivity to rejection and criticism, low self-esteem, and social withdrawal. A typical comorbidity associated with bulimia nervosa is borderline personality disorder, which is marked by impulsivity, intense or chaotic interpersonal relationships, unstable self-image, and extreme emotions, such as intense and inappropriate anger. However, especially in adolescents, it can be very difficult to sort out whether such symptoms are manifestations of an eating disorder, which will subside if the eating disorder is successfully treated, or whether they indicate the existence of a personality disorder. In any case, because so many psychological changes occur during adolescence, most mental health professionals are reluctant to apply the diagnosis of a personality disorder to individuals under the age of 18.

Another phenomenon that can complicate the diagnosis of eating disorders is something that mental health professionals call "diagnostic migration," or the movement of an individual's condition across diagnostic categories from one eating disorder or subtype to another. While a few people migrate from bulimia nervosa to anorexia nervosa, the most frequent change is from the restricting subtype of anorexia nervosa to the binge-purge subtype, reflecting the development of bulimic symptoms. Some individuals gain weight in association with the binge eating, leading to a change in diagnosis from anorexia nervosa restricting subtype or anorexia nervosa binge-purge subtype to bulimia nervosa. In one study, reported in 2002, more than 50% of anorexia nervosa restricting subtype patients, both adolescents and adults, developed bulimic symptoms. It is unknown what factors lead to the development of bulimic symptoms among people with the restricting subtype of anorexia nervosa or what the precise time course of this development is.

The Dangers of Doing Nothing

"After Jody admitted to me that she was bulimic," Shirley says, "I immediately went to the local library to look for resources. I found one book on anorexia. It gave me a bit of insight, but I did not realize at the time that I could not hear what I could not hear. My denial, misconceptions, and misunderstandings about the illness caused me to ignore information that I blithely assumed applied to all others who suffered with disordered eating.

"Jody also insisted that we not tell anyone—she would determine when and to whom her illness was revealed. We told ourselves we were honoring her wishes. I can no longer tell myself that lie. I was as ashamed as Jody was to acknowledge her behavior, and I liked the *results* of her behavior nearly as much as she did—what a trim and pretty daughter I had— such hubris, such ignorance, such humanness. Our silence assured a feeling of isolation in my fears for my daughter, and denial prevented all of us from understanding a lot."

". . . denial prevented all of us from understanding a lot."

Susan echoes these same sentiments regarding her daughter Vanessa's struggle with anorexia nervosa.

"I knew there were problems, but when Vanessa begged me to let her go on a three-week back-packing trip during the summer, I only agreed because she promised she would eat." By the time Vanessa got back from the backpacking trip, however, she'd lost 15 pounds. "The best advice I can offer to other parents is to not stick your head in the ground. Don't think it's a phase that will go away. Follow your gut reactions and, if you're worried, do something about it. It's better for you to be chastised for being an alarmist than it is to let your kid to keep getting sicker because her eating disorder isn't being treated."

"Follow your gut reactions and, if you're worried, do something about it."

Exactly so. Faced with the prospect that your child has an eating disorder, your initial reactions may be alarm, disbelief, denial, anger, bewilderment—in short, a barrage of very powerful feelings, and perhaps even guilt that you're somehow responsible for your child's condition. But with all the feelings that you must contend with at this time, it is critically important that you not let them overwhelm or paralyze you. It is important to remember as well that these disorders are complex and can happen in any family. They occur for reasons that are unknown but that likely involve factors beyond anyone's conscious control. What *is* in your control as a parent, though, is how you deal with the situation now. Confronted with the visible signs or red flags that your child has a serious problem, you can take charge, face the problem head on, and act in your child's best interests by seeking medical help now, just as you would if your child had a serious, purely physical illness. To do otherwise—as Susan says, to "stick your head in the ground"— is to risk facing more serious problems down the road.

Medical Complications of Eating Disorders

Eating disorders are associated with serious medical complications and can be fatal. Most of the complications result from malnutrition or occur as a result of unhealthy weight-control behaviors, like vomiting. Even adolescents who do not meet full criteria for anorexia nervosa or bulimia nervosa but have symptoms of eating disorders may be at risk of developing these complications. Serious though they can be, most of the complications are reversible with nutritional rehabilitation and symptomatic improvement. However, in an adolescent whose growth and development are not yet complete, the medical consequences of eating disorders can be long lasting and irreversible. Particularly worrisome complications for adolescents include growth retardation, pubertal delay or arrest, and impaired acquisition of bone mass.

MEDICAL COMPLICATIONS OF ANOREXIA NERVOSA

The most notable medical complications of anorexia nervosa result from malnutrition. Muscle wastes, cheeks are sunken, and bones protrude through the skin, which itself may be pale, dry, and yellow in color. Body temperature is usually low, and the individual's hands and feet may be cold and blue; he or she will often need multiple layers of clothing to keep warm. Fine downy hair (lanugo) may be present over the arms, back, and face. Scalp hair is dry, listless, and brittle, and there may be evidence of hair loss. Resting pulse and blood pressure are both low—for example, the pulse may be as low as 30 to 40 beats per minute, in contrast to the normal average of between 60 and 100 beats per minute—and changes in both pulse and blood pressure, such as what occurs when the person stands up, may cause dizziness or fainting.

Malnutrition can lead to life-threatening deterioration in the functioning of the heart and cardiovascular system. The effects of malnutrition are often aggravated by imbalances of electrolytes, which are minerals like sodium and potassium needed to maintain physical functions, such as heart rhythm, muscle contraction, and brain function. An electrolyte imbalance is more likely to occur in those who are vomiting or abusing laxatives or diuretics. Individuals who drink excessive amounts of water, either to defray hunger or to falsely elevate body weight before a medical visit, risk low sodium levels (hyponatremia) as well as seizures, coma, and death caused by "water intoxication."

Medical complications such as congestive heart failure can occur during the early phases of refeeding. Bloating and constipation are frequent complaints of patients with anorexia nervosa, indicating delayed gastric emptying and decreased intestinal functioning. Malnutrition also causes the metabolism to slow down, requiring fewer calories to function. Suppression of the bone marrow often occurs, resulting in low white blood cell, red blood cell, and platelet counts. Despite the low white blood cell count, there does not appear to be an increased risk of infection. The major neurological complications of eating disorders are seizures and cerebral atrophy (a reduction in the size of the brain), as well as impairment of attention, concentration, and memory.

The occurrence of anorexia nervosa prior to the completion of an individual's growth interferes with bone development, and some adolescents may never reach their full height. The delay in bone growth is more likely to occur in adolescent boys than in girls because boys grow, on average, for two years longer than girls, whose growth is almost complete by their first menstruation (usually around age 12). In both boys and girls, anorexia nervosa disrupts the hormonal changes that are a normal part of puberty. For example, as we mentioned previously, loss of menstruation, or amenorrhea, is a cardinal feature of anorexia nervosa among girls. Pituitary and ovarian hormones controlling menstruation are all low, and the uterus and ovaries shrink in size. If weight is restored and the girl's menstrual periods resume, however, the ability to conceive should be normal.

. . . loss of menstruation, or amenorrhea, is a cardinal feature of anorexia nervosa among girls.

A serious side effect of prolonged amenorrhea and a low estrogen state is osteopenia, a substantial reduction in bone mass. It is related to poor nutrition, low body weight, estrogen deficiency, and high levels of cortisol (a hormone released by the adrenal glands that is responsible for many of the physiological effects of stress) in the blood stream. The reduction in bone density in females with anorexia nervosa is more severe than it is in those with other conditions associated with amenorrhea and a low estrogen state, suggesting that, in addition to estrogen deficiency, nutritional factors play an important role.

Adolescence is a critical time for bone mass acquisition. Whether or not a young woman will develop osteoporosis in later life depends not only on the rate of bone loss in adulthood, but also on the amount of bone present at skeletal maturity, often referred to as "peak bone mass." Many studies have shown that peak bone mass is achieved toward the end of the second decade of life. A woman who develops anorexia nervosa during adolescence may not reach a normal peak bone mass, placing her at increased risk of developing fractures. This risk may persist for years after recovery from the disorder.

It must also be reiterated that anorexia nervosa has one of the highest mortality rates among psychiatric disorders. The most common causes of death among patients struggling with the disorder are the effects of starvation and suicide. The suicide rate among women with anorexia nervosa is approximately 50 times higher than for women of a similar age in the general population.

MEDICAL COMPLICATIONS OF BULIMIA NERVOSA

Bulimic behaviors, such as self-induced vomiting and laxative and diuretic abuse, can lead directly to dehydration and electrolyte disturbances. Indirectly, they can also cause water retention when these inappropriate behaviors abruptly cease, and the body "overcompensates" by temporarily hanging on to extra water.

A reduced level of potassium in the blood (hypokalemia) is the most common electrolyte disturbance found in patients who vomit, use laxatives, or take diuretics. If the potassium level falls low enough, life-threatening disturbances of heart rhythm can result. Excessive intake of emetics (medications like ipecac, which is used to induce vomiting after accidental poisoning) can cause muscle weakness, congestive heart failure, cardiac arrest, and even death.

Enlargement of the parotid and salivary glands can occur because of binge eating and vomiting. Recurrent vomiting can result in erosion of tooth enamel, gastro-esophageal reflux disease, and inflammation or tears of the esophagus. Some individuals consume so much food during a binge that their stomach or esophagus ruptures. Fortunately, such events are very rare, because they are usually fatal.

Future Prospects

Throughout this chapter, the often grim litany of what is and is not known about eating disorders, and of all that can go wrong as a result once they have developed, belies one critically important point: that most people with these disorders do in fact recover from them, especially if the disorder is recognized and appropriately treated early.

. . . most people with these disorders do in fact recover from them . . .

Among adolescents, up to 70% of those with anorexia nervosa recover over time, and 20% improve but continue to have residual symptoms, while the remainder chronically struggle with the disorder. Relapse, or a return to disordered eating behavior after initially successful treatment, is a common occurrence, and the illness does have one of the highest mortality rates among psychiatric disorders. The mortality rate during adolescence is low, however, and ultimately, the most positive outcomes are seen in individuals between the ages of 12 to 18 with a short duration of illness.

The majority of adolescents and adults with bulimia nervosa also improve over time, with recovery rates ranging from 35% to 75% after five or more years. The illness is rarely fatal, and again, early diagnosis and treatment are important factors in recovery.

The road ahead for you as the parent of an adolescent with an eating disorder will not be easy. You may face months, perhaps even years, of helping your child with all the challenges the illness presents. But together, and with the right interventions from qualified professionals, you can take this battle on and win it.

Valerie says of her daughter Audra, now an adult whose struggle with anorexia nervosa began 15 years ago, "She received good treatment, poor treatment, and no treatment. She has been treated as an outpatient, an inpatient, and institutionalized. She has been incorrectly diagnosed, received drugs she did not need, and lost in between the cracks of systems that were not trained to recognize eating disorders. Because of her anorexia, she has heart irregularities, osteoporosis, and has lost kidney function. Since her release from the hospital, daily life has been a round of trips to numerous doctors and will continue that way until her psychiatrist thinks she has been in remission long enough to spread the doctor visits further apart.

"Still, after all that, our daughter has achieved a fairly normal life. She has gotten married, has a daughter, attends family functions, goes to church, and would like to have another child in a few years. She sometimes talks about the possibility of returning

". . . getting the right treatment has helped her to want to keep on going. The dreams are alive."

to school and becoming a physical therapist. She struggles daily with her weight and her willingness to eat. She knows that this is something that will be with her for the rest of her life, but getting the right treatment has helped her to want to keep on going. The dreams are alive."

Phil's mother Cathleen adds: "If your child is recovering from anorexia nervosa, the most important thing a parent can do is to make sure they maintain the 'goal' weight set by the doctor. Reaching [that weight] was tough for Phil, but the closer he got to it, the better his brain functioned, and he eventually started to understand that going back to a low weight at any time would be dangerous because it could start the cycle all over again. So we will hold on to that for a long time so that he can keep thinking clearly and stay focused on his recovery."

Chapter Three

Getting the Right Treatment for Your Child: Therapy, Medication, and More

F acing the possibility that your child may have an eating disorder is only the first step toward getting him or her help. The next step is to find the right kind of help, a task that can feel overwhelming at first. Where do you start? Since eating disorders involve both psychological issues as well as physical complications, should you initially approach a general practitioner or consult a psychologist? Or should you find someone who specializes in eating disorders? If the diagnosis of an eating disorder is confirmed, what will the treatment for it involve and how long will it take? Does your child need to be hospitalized? How much will treatment cost, and will your insurance cover it?

All of these are important considerations when taking the initial step toward finding treatment for an adolescent with an eating disorder. To help you make informed choices as you and your child go through the treatment process, this chapter surveys the various settings (e.g., hospitalization, outpatient), approaches (e.g., psychotherapy and medication), and relapse prevention methods that you may encounter along the way. Guidance on how to navigate the health care system is offered as well.

Finding Treatment: Where to Begin

All eating disorder experts recommend that the first step is to make an appointment with a general practitioner, ideally someone your child knows and trusts, such as his or her pediatrician or your family doctor. A medical assessment will be necessary to determine your teen's general physical condition as well as to rule out other causes for symptoms like rapid weight loss or low pulse rate. It is also crucial in determining whether immediate intensive intervention, such as hospitalization, is needed. Necessary as this assessment is, however, it is sometimes inconclusive: Routine physical tests, such as blood work, are often entirely normal, and can be of limited use in establishing the diagnosis. Therefore, because it is so critical to recognize and treat these diseases early, ask the physician for a referral to someone who specializes in eating disorders, just to be sure. As Audra's mother Valerie says, "It has been my experience that some members of the regular medical community are not knowledgeable in the recognition or treatment of eating disorders. By the time they recognize a problem, the patient can already be in a life-threatening situation. If your insurance company won't cover the consultation, find a specialist and make the appointment yourself, and then be prepared to pay for it yourself."

. . . ask the physician for a referral to someone who specializes in eating disorders . . .

The prospect of finding a qualified specialist on your own can seem daunting, but there are numerous organizations—such as local mental health associations and professional psychiatric or psychological organizations—that can offer assistance and referrals for providers in your area. Another option is to contact your health insurance carrier for a referral, which will also ensure that treatment will be covered under your policy. Additionally, there are many national eating disorders associations that can aid in finding treatment. Their names, phone numbers, and addresses are listed in the Resources section at the end of this book.

If the doctor does positively confirm that your child has an eating disorder and gives you a referral to a specialist, don't make the call with the expectation that your child will be able to see the specialist the next day. Because of the limited number of professionals specializing in eating disorders, some treatment providers have substantial waiting lists for their services, and you may have to wait weeks, perhaps even months, before one of them can see your child. The delay, combined with the worry about what is wrong with your child, can increase tensions within your family. Donna explains:

"Because Chelsey was exhibiting signs that made us suspect she had an eating disorder, my husband Eric and I insisted she see the family physician who'd been treating her since she was a little girl. She fought it, but we wouldn't budge, so she eventually went. Once there, the doctor recommended having an evaluation at a specialized center for eating disorders. Eric and I were relieved because we thought she'd get the help she needed right away, but it took two whole months for her to even be seen by someone there. During the waiting period, we had to physically monitor her, which really put a strain on our relationship with her. She just couldn't understand that we were doing it to help her. Anyway, once she was finally evaluated, the specialist at the center recommended inpatient treatment, which Chelsey adamantly refused, so I agreed to drive her there everyday as an outpatient on the condition that if she lost even one ounce, she'd have

"She just couldn't understand that we were doing it to help her."

to be admitted as an inpatient. It wasn't an ideal situation for any of us, but at least she was finally getting some help."

What Does Treatment Involve?

As is the case for almost all serious illnesses, the treatment of eating disorders is both an art and a science. Science provides the facts—about what treatments are known to work, what treatments are known to be ineffective, and what are the complications of different treatments. Unfortunately, the scientific basis for the treatment of eating disorders, especially among adolescents, is far from complete. The art lies in combining the incomplete scientific base with a sense of what is a good "fit" for a particular adolescent who lives in a particular family in a particular community, and in constructing a treatment approach that will be acceptable and effective. The practitioner's experience and his or her ability to work well with the adolescent and the family are crucial elements of the art of treatment.

Since the 1990s, a growing consensus has developed among health professionals and among the organizations that pay for treatment, like insurance companies and the government, that all medical treatment should be "evidence-based." That is, the only treatments that should be used (and paid for) are ones that have been proven to be effective by rigorous scientific studies. In theory, this is an excellent principle. However, in many areas of medicine, including eating disorders, the "evidence base" is very small, making it virtually impossible for providers to confidently make evidence-based recommendations. There are no scientific studies to indicate the optimal treatment for adolescents with eating disorders, in terms of when treatment should begin, where treatment should be administered, or who should provide it. Therefore, treatment recommendations for adolescents with eating disorders, including those treatments we will describe in this chapter, are based more on experience and on extending to adolescents the somewhat better developed knowledge about adults.

In general, experts agree that therapy should begin as soon as possible after the diagnosis has been established, with the treatment provider(s), parents, and patient working together to individualize treatment. Unfortunately, as Donna's story illustrated, the setting for treatment as well as the optimal provider is likely to be determined, at least partially, by availability.

A comprehensive plan to address all of the complexities of the disease should incorporate medical, physical, and nutritional monitoring, psychotherapeutic intervention, and, if necessary, medication management. A variety of different professionals, including physicians (psychiatrists, primary care providers, or adolescent medicine specialists), psychologists, social workers, and nutritionists familiar with syndromes like anorexia nervosa, bulimia nervosa, and binge eating disorder can play key roles in the effectiveness of treatment. Therefore, it may take time to find the right treatment plan and providers that best suit your child as well as the rest of your family. In addition, because of the relative lack of scientific certainty about what constitutes the "best treatment," it is important for you to be aware of the treatment options and to use your own judgment about what is right for your child and your family.

It is also important to keep in mind that effective treatment is built, at least in part, on an establishment of trust between your child and the treatment team. This trust doesn't happen overnight, and most of the parents interviewed for this book stressed the long time it took to find a provider or providers who had a "good fit" with their child. Among the challenges to

Professional Guidelines for Assessing and Treating Eating Disorders

Several professional organizations have now developed guidelines to help practitioners assess and treat adolescent eating disorders. One of them is the Society for Adolescent Medicine (SAM), whose members include professionals in medicine, nursing, psychology, public health, social work, nutrition, education, and law. Published in 2003, the SAM guidelines established five major positions regarding the treatment of adolescents with eating disorders:

1. Diagnosis should be considered in the context of normal adolescent growth and development, since adolescents, especially younger ones, may have significant health risks associated with dysfunctional weight control practices, even though they do not meet full *DSM-IV* **criteria.**

2. Treatment should be initiated at lower symptom levels for adolescents than for adults.

3. Nutritional management should reflect the patient's age, pubertal stage, and physical activity level.

4. Family-based treatment should be considered an important part of treatment for most adolescents, and mental health services should address the psychological dimensions of eating disorders, the developmental challenges of adolescence, and possible coexisting psychiatric conditions.

5. The assessment and treatment of adolescents are best accomplished by a treatment team that is knowledgeable about normal adolescent physical and psychological development. Hospitalization would be necessary in the presence of severe malnutrition, physiologic instability, severe mental health disturbance, or failure of outpatient treatment.

Another organization, the American Academy of Pediatrics (AAP), also published a statement in 2003 about the treatment of adolescents with eating disorders and about the role that primary care providers now play in the identification and treatment of these disorders. The AAP's statement emphasized the unique position of primary care pediatricians—as part of routine, preventive health care—to detect the onset of eating disorders and to stop their progression at the earliest stages of the illness. Additionally, because of their existing relationship with a patient, primary care givers already have an established, trusting relationship with the patient and the family, and usually have the necessary knowledge and skills to monitor health. The AAP policy statement also advocated rapid and aggressive treatment of eating disorders, and noted that hospitalization might be required in the case of emerging medical or psychiatric needs or in the event that a patient fails to respond to intensive outpatient treatment.

In January 2004, the United Kingdom's National Institute for Clinical Excellence (NICE) published guidelines that make recommendations for the identification, treatment, and management of anorexia nervosa, bulimia nervosa, and eating disorders not otherwise specified (including binge eating disorder). The guidelines also contain recommendations regarding treatment of adolescents with anorexia nervosa and bulimia nervosa; some of their general recommendations are as follows:

1. Family members, including siblings, should normally be included in the treatment of children and adolescents with eating disorders.

2. In children and adolescents with eating disorders, growth and development should be closely monitored. Where development is delayed or growth is stunted despite adequate nutrition, pediatric advice should be sought.

3. Health care professionals assessing children and adolescents with eating disorders should be alert to indicators of abuse (emotional, physical, and sexual) and should remain so throughout treatment.

4. The right to confidentiality of children and adolescents with eating disorders should be respected.

overcome will be the fairly heady resistance that your child will likely exhibit to treatment in the first place. Since people with eating disorders initially assume that the ultimate goal of treatment is to make them gain weight, they are reluctant to confide in treatment providers or to stay in treatment for more than a short time. After one or two sessions, for example, your daughter might tell you she no longer needs to see a therapist or that she can stop the disordered-eating behavior on her own.

But in fact, even with treatment, it can take a long time for someone to recover from an eating disorder. As a parent, you can play an important part in sustaining the resolve, both your child's and your own, to give the treatment process and your child's providers enough time to work and to show positive results. At the same time, however, you should remain vigilant: If after a reasonable period you see that your child isn't progressing (e.g., is still losing weight or continuing to show signs of binge eating/purging), it is may be necessary to search for other approaches and providers.

Additionally, many programs include family therapy sessions, which can seem intimidating to many parents. As Audra's mother Valerie says, "We love our daughter very much and had spent a long time attending individual, family, and group therapy. We were willing to do anything that might help her. For years, we had listened to one mental health professional after another tell us that Audra's problems were our fault, so we always thought we had to shoulder that enormous burden of guilt. When our daughter began seeing a therapist who specialized in treating eating disorders, the best thing for us as parents was that we were finally told we had not caused her illness. You can't imagine how relieved we were to find out we were not to blame."

In fact, emerging evidence suggests that family therapy is an effective intervention for treating anorexia nervosa and may also be useful for bulimia nervosa. Therefore, if the treatment team recommends family therapy sessions, don't be reluctant to attend because you fear you will constantly be under attack or accused of causing your child's problems. As discussed in Chapter 2, the fundamental causes of eating disorders are unknown. A good therapist will avoid getting into the

A good therapist will avoid getting into the "who's to blame" game . . .

"who's to blame" game, and instead focus on your child's recovery and on your participation as a vital component in that process. Cathleen's experience with the treatment her son Phil received illustrates this point:

"When Phil was admitted to the eating disorders clinic, the doctor and others there said that it didn't matter why he got sick. All that mattered at that point was that his health was restored. Sometimes you never quite know why a child gets sick, and it can hold you back if you focus too much on that aspect of treatment. The first priority is that your son gets well, which also takes the pressure off of him because he isn't constantly being bombarded with the 'why's.' Looking forward instead of looking back can make all the difference in your child's recovery process."

Once you have identified a potential treatment provider, it will be helpful to ask him or her some questions, such as the following:

- What is the diagnosis of my child's eating problem?

- How many teenagers with this sort of problem have you treated?

- Have you identified any other important emotional or psychological problems, like depression or substance use? (See Chapter 2, pp. 46–50)

- What treatment setting is most appropriate (inpatient, outpatient, or an intermediate level of care)?

- What type of psychological counseling do you recommend?

- Do you recommend the use of any medications?

- How often will you see my child?

- To what degree will our family be involved in treatment, and will information about my child's progress be shared with me?

- How is my child's physical condition going to be monitored (including who will weigh my child, and how often?)

For most of these questions, there are no absolutely "correct" answers. Rather, they provide a basis for beginning an important dialogue with the person who will be helping to care for your child. It is very important that you and the treatment provider understand each other's perspective and that you are comfortable with the provider's plan to treat the eating disorder. (The National Eating Disorders Association, or NEDA, has posted on its Web site two excellent lists of similar questions that you can also ask treatment providers. Both complete lists can be accessed by logging on to www.nationaleatingdisorders.org.)

It is very important that you and the treatment provider understand each other's perspective

Once you've found a specialist or treatment program that suits your child's needs, the sequence of specific interventions will be determined, in part, by the need to address the more acute and medically serious problems first. Several important goals to achieve, in order of decreasing urgency, include

- Correct potentially life-threatening health complications (e.g., heart irregularities, low blood pressure, dehydration)

- Minimize risks of self-harm, such as suicidal behavior

- Restore weight to normal

- Develop normal eating behavior and eliminate binge eating and purging

- Address psychological and psychosocial issues (e.g., low self-esteem, body image distortion, problems in interpersonal relationships)

- Maintain long-term recovery

Where Will Treatment Take Place?

Where and how your child will be treated will depend largely on the severity of the physical and psychological symptoms of the eating disorder and any related problems. If, for example, your daughter's health is compromised to the point that she has potentially life-threatening medical complications, she would first need to be physically stabilized before other interventions can be considered. But if she has been diagnosed early enough so that hospitalization isn't required, outpatient therapy would likely fit her needs as well as those of your family. Close medical monitoring on an inpatient basis is warranted especially for individuals whose anorexia nervosa has reached an advanced stage. Appropriately trained health care professionals can usually treat bulimia nervosa on an outpatient basis, but some individuals with this disorder need to be monitored for potential medical complications as well. The various options are further explained below.

Medical Hospitalization

In the most severe cases of eating disorders, short-term hospitalization in a medical unit (sometimes in an intensive care unit) is required to stabilize and then monitor your child medically. Vital signs (blood pressure, heart rate and rhythm) will be watched closely and the acute physical effects of malnutrition and of binge eating and purging will be treated with fluids and medications. If the patient is underweight, refeeding will be initiated orally or, if necessary, by means of intravenous or nasogastric feedings. Hospitalization usually lasts anywhere from three to ten days, depending on how severe the medical problems are and how the patient responds to rehabilitative efforts.

Inpatient Psychiatric Treatment

Inpatient psychiatric care differs from short-term medical hospitalization in that, once a patient is medically stabilized, treatment efforts can focus more intensively on behavioral and psychological issues. Most inpatient psychiatric units are located in a general hospital and often provide care not only for patients with eating disorders but also for patients with other psychiatric problems. Meals are closely supervised, and intensive individual and/or group psychological treatment is provided. Conditions that may coexist with the eating disorder (e.g., depression, anxiety disorder, or obsessive-compulsive disorder) are carefully assessed, and appropriate treatments initiated. Most eating disorder inpatient units have 24-hour clinical support available from physicians, psychiatrists, psychologists, and nutritionists. The average length of stay is one to four weeks, depending on the patient's response to treatment and on how much insurance and other financial support is available (see the section "Navigating the Health Care System" in this chapter). For some families, inpatient treatment works; for others, it doesn't.

"We had been in counseling for a year when Linda relapsed," Kay says of the initial treatment they were pursuing for her daughter, who struggled with bulimia nervosa. "During that relapse, the counselor realized Linda needed something more. She discussed sending her to a psychiatrist about fifty miles away, but then I found a large university that had an eating disorder unit. Even though it was over eighty miles away, I thought it looked like a better option because it had a whole treatment team."

Linda was hospitalized twice for a total of nine weeks. "It was inpatient," Kay says. "But as I found out after the first hospitalization, they merely stabilized her medically. They did provide therapy, nutritional counseling, and helped us find a therapist in our area. However, they really didn't give Linda the tools she needed to help her deal with situations after she got home. I would never do a hospital-type setting again. I think a small residential setting would be better. It would be more personalized. The big university hospital had too many doctors involved, and you received too much conflicting information. Things were always changing, and we weren't informed. They also had no informational classes for parents, and we felt totally excluded from her treatment."

Conversely, Cathleen has nothing but praise for the treatment her son Phil received in a large, university-affiliated eating disorders unit. "The care he got was exceptional, and the doctors always kept me informed of what was going on with his treatment. Being the only boy on the unit also worked out fine for him. Some guys might have hated it, but because all the women there wanted to get better, it was a very positive and encouraging environment for Phil. Everyone was very supportive and nurtured him and built him up. As much as he hated being in the hospital, I know their support—in addition to that of the doctors—really helped him."

Residential Care

Residential care can be described as inpatient treatment on a smaller scale and in a less medical and more "home-like"

"As much as he hated being in the hospital, I know their support . . . really helped him."

environment than large hospitals. Treatment for children and teens usually includes individual and group therapy sessions, creative therapy (e.g., art, music, writing), academic services, nutrition classes, and recreational activities. The average stay in a residential care program can last several months and the cost can be expensive (sometimes as much as $1,500 or more per day).

Both inpatient treatment and residential care may be crucial for adolescents whose physical states are at the critical stage, but the prospect of watching your child being "locked up," as one mother put it, can certainly be very upsetting.

"There is nothing you want more than for your child to be home with you," says Diane, whose daughter Megan was treated for anorexia nervosa. "But as I found out the hard way, you can't 'police' them 24 hours a day, nor do you have the skills to deal with all of the complex aspects of the disease that's overwhelmed them. And I have to admit that, once my daughter was finally admitted to a long-term residential care facility, I felt a tremendous sense of relief about not being in the position of constantly having to try to 'save' her. I could just be a parent again. I was able to visit her on a weekly basis, which gave me the opportunity to be supportive and encouraging instead of being the nasty witch who forced her to eat or tried to stop her from doing 300 sit-ups in the middle of the night."

Partial Hospitalization Program (PHP) or Day Hospital Care

Often recommended for those making a transition from an inpatient or residential facility, PHP is a daily program, usually lasting 4 to 8 hours, that provides structured eating situations and active treatment interventions while allowing the individual to live at home and participate in certain school activities. Such programs may also be recommended as the first intervention for adolescents who need close supervision but not the 24-hour care provided in hospital and residential settings.

Intensive Outpatient Therapy (IOP)

IOP requires patients to come to an outpatient clinic for several hours on several days per week. While at the clinic, the patient will attend therapy sessions (often group therapy) and, in many cases, have supervised meals.

Outpatient Care

Except in life-threatening situations, outpatient therapy is the most widely used form of treatment for adolescents with eating disorders. Sessions are often scheduled once a week, but may occur more frequently for patients who need more intensive help, or less frequently for patients who are improving and can maintain more normal eating habits with less intensive supervision. The teen is able to live at home and attend school but consults regularly with members of his or her treatment team (e.g., physician, psychotherapist, and dietitian or nutritionist). Family therapy sessions can also be an integral part of outpatient treatment.

Family therapy sessions can also be an integral part of outpatient treatment.

Psychological Treatments

Psychotherapy, or psychological counseling, is an integral component of treatment for eating disorders. Research studies of adults, especially of those with bulimia nervosa, have shown that such psychological approaches are clearly useful. Unfortunately, only a very small number of studies have focused specifically on how well such treatments work for adolescents with eating disorders. In recent years, the National Institutes of Health (NIH) has recognized the critical need for more research on the treatment of eating disorders in general, and among adolescents in particular, and there is good reason to hope that much more knowledge will emerge in the next decade. But, as we discussed at the beginning of this chapter, the "evidence base" regarding what treatments are of proven effectiveness is extremely limited at present. Therefore, general treatment recommendations for adolescents with eating disorders must be constructed by extending the modest amount of scientific information available from studies of adults and from the clinical experience of specialists in the field.

If your daughter has been diagnosed with anorexia nervosa or bulimia nervosa, the types of psychological interventions available to both her and your family during the recovery process can include individual psychotherapy, family therapy, and group therapy. Which type of treatment she receives will depend not only on her needs but also on the availability of knowledgeable practitioners and their experience with different treatment approaches. In the next section, we will briefly describe what to expect from each of these therapies. Then we will summarize the limited amount of information available about which of these approaches may be most effective for particular types of eating disorders.

Individual Psychotherapy

Individual psychotherapy ("talk therapy") is a private, one-on-one intervention that occurs between a trained therapist (such as a psychiatrist, psychologist, or social worker) and a patient, usually once or twice a week. Several different theoretical approaches underlie and direct what the therapist does and talks about in individual psychotherapy. We will describe the major theoretical perspectives, but we should emphasize that, while they may seem quite different from each other on paper, in practice, many therapists combine elements from them all.

PSYCHODYNAMICALLY ORIENTED, SUPPORTIVE PSYCHOTHERAPY

Although no reliable statistics are available, it is likely that this form of individual therapy is the approach most commonly employed for adolescents with any kind of psychological problem, including an eating disorder. This approach has its historical roots in the psychoanalytic traditions of Sigmund Freud and his disciples, and it exists in many varieties. Their common thread is a focus on the patient's inner psychological experience, based on the assumption that the patient's unresolved psychological conflicts and uncertainties produce emotional upheaval and lead to behavioral disturbances, including eating disorders.

One of the most appealing aspects of this form of individual psychotherapy for a person with an eating disorder is its one-on-one format, which provides a "safe" environment where feelings can be shared without worrying about who might approve or disapprove of what is being said. Adolescents with eating disorders may be reluctant to express themselves honestly at home, at school, or in social circles for fear others will disapprove of what they might say. Low self-esteem can cause them to remain silent because they think their opinions don't warrant attention. For a teen with anorexia nervosa who feels inadequate or unable to discuss her problems, refusing to eat is a powerful option for expressing herself without having to say a single word. But in sessions with a

. . . refusing to eat is a powerful option for expressing herself without having to say a single word.

therapist, who is supposed to be an objective, nonjudgmental observer, a reticent teen has the opportunity to talk openly about troubling relationships at home, social pressures at school, and other factors that can contribute to the development and maintenance of her eating disorder. Additionally, understanding and confronting the roots of feelings such as inadequacy or worthlessness can enable her to eventually find other ways of coping with life's problems besides waging a fierce battle against the natural needs of her body.

The effectiveness of individual psychotherapy, especially one using the psychodynamic approach, depends on the bond formed between the patient and the therapist, and it normally takes a while before they actually "click." It's important to re-emphasize this point, especially if your daughter comes to you after only one session and tells you she hates her therapist and doesn't want to go back anymore. This may be a natural response because she fears the therapist is there to make her fat by taking away her "safety net," which is the disordered eating behavior. Try to talk her through this resistance by telling her as gently as possible that getting to know someone doesn't happen right away. It can even help to remind her of a teacher she originally disliked but eventually came to respect or of a classmate she first thought of as "dorky" who wound up becoming a close friend. By doing so, you can help her understand that she needs to give the therapist several more chances before giving up. As one mother put it, "It took my daughter a few months to understand that her therapist wasn't the enemy, the anorexia was. Once she finally got it, she actually started looking forward to her therapy sessions

"It took my daughter a few months to understand that her therapist wasn't the enemy, the anorexia was."

and would come home chattering about anything that popped into her head. It was quite an amazing difference from the silent, sullen girl who had previously referred to her therapist as 'that big jerk.'"

Even if the fit between patient and therapist is excellent, you should be aware of a worry some experts have about the psychodynamic approach to eating disorders. There is no scientific proof that anorexia nervosa or bulimia nervosa is, in fact, caused by "underlying" psychological problems, or, even if it is, that resolving them inevitably leads to the resolution of the eating disorder. It is certainly important for any therapy to address problems with self-esteem, and to help the youngster understand what he or she is going through. But it is also important that the symptoms of the eating disorder, including weight loss, binge eating, and purging, be frequently monitored and addressed in some way.

In other words, as noted previously, if your daughter doesn't seem to be progressing after a certain period of time with this treatment (indeed, with *any* form of treatment), you have the option of finding someone else whom she might feel more comfortable with or who takes a different approach. Several parents interviewed for this book emphasized just this point. "My advice to other parents is to always remember you have choices," Susan said. "I wasn't pleased with the way Vanessa's therapy was going, but didn't say anything because I thought, 'Well, she's in the hands of a professional. They must know better than I do about what she needs.' As it turned out, the therapy wasn't a good fit at all, my daughter completely relapsed, and I kept kicking myself for not following my instincts. If your kid isn't getting better, it's imperative to keep trying to find someone else until she does."

INTERPERSONAL PSYCHOTHERAPY

Interpersonal psychotherapy, often referred to as IPT, also shares its origins with psychodynamic psychotherapy, but differs in several important respects. IPT was developed in the 1980s as a short-term (12 to 16 sessions) treatment for depression among adults, and focuses primarily on the individual's social functioning. The therapist is quite active in helping the patient identify problem areas, such as "role transitions," and uses several specific techniques, including role playing, to help the patient develop new methods of dealing with his or her interpersonal relationships.

In research studies of depressed adults, IPT has been found to be very helpful, so much so that it has been adapted specifically for adolescents struggling with depression (renamed IPT-A) and, again, has been clearly demonstrated to be effective. IPT-A focuses on several difficulties of obvious importance to adolescents, including separation from parents, relationships with members of the opposite sex, and peer pressures. It would appear to have much to offer in the treatment of adolescents with eating disorders, as its methods are well described, it addresses interpersonal issues that many adolescents with eating disorders struggle with, and it is effective for depression, a condition that commonly affects teens with these syndromes. In fact, IPT has been used in several research studies to treat adults with bulimia nervosa, with at least one study showing specific evidence of its effectiveness with this group.

COGNITIVE-BEHAVIORAL THERAPY

Cognitive-behavioral therapy (CBT) was developed for adults with depression in the 1960s and is based on the theory that persistent but maladaptive thinking patterns are key contributors to emotional disturbances. A substantial body of scientific evidence supports the effectiveness of CBT for the treatment of depression and anxiety disorders, both in adults and in adolescents. Beginning in the 1970s, CBT was tailored specifically to the treatment of eating disorders.

Beginning in the 1970s, CBT was tailored specifically to the treatment of eating disorders.

As the name implies, cognitive-behavioral therapy focuses on "cognition" (e.g., one's views and perceptions of oneself) and "behavior" (e.g., one's reactions to those perceptions), with the aim of correcting those ingrained patterns of cognition and behavior that may be contributing to one's illness. The cognitive part of CBT helps people to identify unrealistic thoughts or habitually pessimistic attitudes and to reframe them in more realistic or optimistic terms. The behavioral part of CBT helps people to change the way they react to the world around them by developing better coping strategies for dealing with their interpersonal relationships and their illness.

As applied to eating disorders, the primary importance of CBT lies in its exploration of the individual's idealized body weight and shape and of his or her behavioral reactions to that idealization. For example, if your daughter fears gaining weight, she might start to restrict her food intake in rigid and unrealistic ways, such as by fasting. However, the fast then leaves her completely starved, both physiologically and psychologically, which in turn leads to a voracious need to satisfy her hunger through binge eating. The episode of binge eating is then followed by purging (e.g., vomiting, laxative abuse, or diuretic abuse) as she attempts to reduce shame and anxiety about possibly gaining weight from the binge. Additionally, binge eating and purging can cause distress and low self-esteem, thereby fostering conditions that lead to more dietary restraint followed once again by binge eating.

To interrupt this vicious cycle, CBT applies cognitive and behavioral procedures designed to modify the individual's unrealistic attitudes about shape and weight and to help her both resume regular eating patterns that include the consumption of previously avoided foods and develop constructive skills for coping with high-risk situations that might trigger binge eating and purging. These same procedures can also help to prevent the individual from relapsing back into her bulimic behaviors at the conclusion of treatment.

Family Therapy

As the name suggests, family therapy involves bringing members of the patient's family together for group sessions. Depending on the therapist's particular training, the treatment may use different approaches, but its overall goals tend to be the same across methods: to identify and change the patterns that may contribute to and/or arise from a teen's eating disorder, and to open lines of communication and teach everyone coping skills for dealing with the illness. Other goals may include strengthening family bonds, reducing conflict in the home, and improving empathy among family members.

One of the most promising family therapies developed to treat adolescents with anorexia nervosa (and now also being explored as a treatment for adolescents with bulimia nervosa) is referred to as the "Maudsley method." (Several excellent books have been written about this method, including James Lock and Daniel Le Grange's *Help Your Teenager Beat an Eating Disorder* [2005].) Developed at the Maudsley Hospital in London, this form of family therapy was specifically designed for adolescent patients and is quite unlike other, more generic family-based programs. Instead of focusing on the psychological roots of disordered eating, the Maudsley method is aimed specifically at addressing eating problems and eating behavior and emphasizes the participation of the family as a vital component to the success of treatment. There are two main phases of treatment.

The first phase focuses on weight restoration and attempts to change behavior by initially transferring control of the patient's eating to the parents. In other words, you as the parent will be responsible for "refeeding" your child. While the term *refeeding* might conjure up images of having to tie your daughter down and force-feed her, in this case it simply means using food as medicine you administer to help your child get well, just as you would give her antibiotics if she had a severe infection.

During this phase, food and eating behavior are also explored as part of the family dynamic. For example, you might be asked to bring a picnic to a therapy session. While you and your family arrange place settings, dole out food, and then eat, the therapist (who does not partake of the meal) asks questions about who plans the meals at home, who buys the groceries, who prepares the food, who serves the food, and so on. Once the picnic is over, the therapist can then offer observations about ways in which your family communicated, socialized, formed allegiances, and dealt with other issues revolving around food behavior during the meal. These insights can help you to understand the effects the disease has on your daughter, as well as on the rest of your family, and to learn how all of you can work together to help her reach the goal weight set by her doctor.

Once your daughter's weight has been restored, the second phase of the Maudsley method begins. During this phase, responsibility for maintaining the weight is gradually transferred

> . . . food and eating behavior are also explored as part of the family dynamic.

to your daughter and treatment begins to focus more on general family and individual concerns, with the therapist providing problem-solving skills for both your daughter and your family to help prevent the recurrence of anorexia nervosa.

Group Therapy

Another therapeutic option is group therapy. In this method, group sessions are usually led by a mental health care professional (e.g., psychiatrist, psychologist, social worker), who facilitates a dialogue among patients trying to recover from similar diseases. In the case of eating disorders, a group therapy session might consist of discussions about body image, the importance of food (both psychologically and physically), social problems, or other issues that the group leader might think need addressing. Group therapy sessions are commonly used in more intensive treatment settings, like hospitals and day programs, and may involve preparing and eating meals.

Since many people with eating disorders tend to isolate themselves and avoid speaking out about their problems or feelings, group therapy may not work for everybody. Still, as part of a comprehensive treatment program, it can help some adolescents to share their feelings with others who understand what they're going through. The outcome seems to depend on who is leading the sessions and the individuals involved, but no research has been conducted to validate the ultimate effectiveness of this therapy.

What's the Right Psychological Treatment for Your Child?

Among the various psychological approaches used to treat eating disorders, which will work best for your child's particular type of eating problem? Regrettably, a clear and straightfor-

ward answer to this question is simply not available. Different youngsters appear to respond differently to
different treatments, and scientific
knowledge about what works best is

Different youngsters appear to respond differently to different treatments . . .

very limited, especially for adolescents. In the following discussion, we will attempt to provide some guidance on this question, often drawing on the modest evidence that has been
established with regard to leading treatments for adults with
eating disorders. But, as we have emphasized several times, it is
important for you to assess this information in light of your
own family's and child's needs, and not to be afraid to make
changes in a given treatment if it isn't working.

FOR ANOREXIA NERVOSA

Only a few studies have scientifically compared the utility of
different forms of psychotherapy for adolescents with anorexia
nervosa, and these have focused primarily on the Maudsley
method of family therapy. The good news is that these studies
are uniformly encouraging about the effectiveness of this approach. Most of the adolescents treated did very well, with a
majority returning to a normal or near-normal weight while in
treatment and sustaining their recovery after treatment ended.
The results of these studies have led most experts to recommend this approach as the first intervention to try for adolescents with anorexia nervosa.

However, a major unanswered question about the Maudsley
method is how well it compares to other methods of treatment,
especially individual psychotherapy. The studies that are available either have not examined that question or are too small for
us to be fully confident of the results. For example, CBT is clearly
helpful for adolescents with other problems such as depression,

is the treatment of choice for adults with bulimia nervosa, and appears to be useful for adults with anorexia nervosa. So, there is good reason to think that CBT would be helpful for adolescents with anorexia nervosa. But until the results of more studies are available, the Maudsley family method should be considered the leading treatment for adolescents with anorexia nervosa.

FOR BULIMIA NERVOSA

No adequate scientific studies of psychological treatments for adolescents with bulimia nervosa have been published, although the Maudsley family therapy approach as adapted for this group is currently being examined. In the meantime, recommendations are based primarily on what is known about the treatment of bulimia nervosa in adults, for whom CBT is widely considered the treatment of choice. CBT has been intensively evaluated in a large number of randomized controlled trials (studies in which the participants are randomly assigned to a treatment group or a control group) involving adults with bulimia nervosa and has been shown, on average, to have eliminated binge eating and purging in roughly 30% to 50% of the patients in these studies. The percentage reduction in binge eating and purging across all patients treated with CBT was typically 80% or more. Also, dysfunctional dieting decreased, attitudes about body shape and weight improved, and there was usually a reduction in the level of anxiety and depression, as well as greater self-esteem and social functioning. The use of CBT in adults has also been found to be equal or superior to all the treatments with which it has been compared, including IPT and psychodynamically oriented psychotherapy.

The effectiveness of CBT in treating adolescents with bulimia nervosa is unproven, but it has been used successfully to treat teens for conditions that can coexist with an eating disorder. It has, for example, resulted in faster remission of adolescent depression than that produced by alternative forms of psychotherapy, including family and supportive therapy. There is also evidence of the effectiveness of CBT in children with anxiety disorders, both at the end of treatment and for a number of years afterward. If similarly applied to the treatment of bulimia nervosa in teens, the procedures that comprise CBT are likely to produce similarly positive results.

. . . CBT in treating adolescents with bulimia nervosa is unproven, but it has been used successfully to treat teens for conditions that can coexist with an eating disorder.

IPT, while not quite as effective as CBT for adults with bulimia nervosa, is nonetheless useful. And again, it has been successfully used to treat teens with depression, which in turn suggests it as a promising approach to the treatment of adolescent bulimia nervosa.

FOR OTHER ADOLESCENT EATING DISORDERS

As discussed in Chapter 2, the majority of adolescents with eating disorders do not meet the *DSM-IV* diagnostic criteria for anorexia nervosa or bulimia nervosa but instead fall into the category called eating disorder not otherwise specified—in other words, the "EDNOS grab bag." Treatment for those in this category must therefore be able to accommodate a wide range of eating problems. One recently developed approach that shows promise for EDNOS patients is a form of CBT with a "transdiagnostic model" of eating disorders, where specific therapeutic interventions are matched to particular clinical features of the eating disorder, rather than to a heterogeneous diagnostic category. The flexibility of this enhanced CBT could be especially useful in treating adolescents in the EDNOS category.

According to the National Institute of Diabetes and Digestive and Kidney Diseases, researchers are still trying to determine which treatment is the most helpful in controlling binge eating disorder, technically an EDNOS illness in the *DSM-IV*. For people who are overweight, a weight-loss program that also offers treatment for eating disorders might be the best choice. Although not yet assessed among adolescents, psychological interventions that would seem to be particularly helpful for binge eating disorder are CBT and IPT. With more research, other interventions (such as medication) might also prove successful in treating this disorder.

Medication

As a parent, it's likely you'll need to deal with the issue of medication while your child is in treatment for an eating disorder. The most common type of "psychotropic" (mind- or mood-altering) medications prescribed for individuals with eating disorders are antidepressants such as those listed in Table 3.

. . . it's likely you'll need to deal with the issue of medication while your child is in treatment for an eating disorder.

A number of studies of antidepressants have been conducted in anorexia nervosa, evaluating fluoxetine (Prozac), which is a selective serotonin reuptake inhibitor (SSRI), and amitriptyline (Elavil) and clomipramine (Anafranil), which are tricyclic antidepressants (TCAs). But nothing more than a slight therapeutic effect, at most, was reported. Because antidepressants have proven useful in treating other conditions that can

Table 3
Antidepressants

Type of antidepressant	Generic name	Usual brand name
Selective serotonin reuptake inhibitors (SSRIs)	citalopram	Celexa
	escitalopram	Lexapro
	fluoxetine	Prozac
	fluvoxamine	Luvox
	paroxetine	Paxil
	sertraline	Zoloft
Other "modern" antidepressants	bupropion	Wellbutrin
	duloxetine	Cymbalta
	mirtazapine	Remeron
	venlafaxine	Effexor
Tricyclic antidepressants (TCAs)	amitriptyline	Elavil
	clomipramine	Anafranil
	desipramine	Norpramin
	doxepin	Sinequan
	imipramine	Tofranil
	maprotiline	Ludiomil
	nortriptyline	Pamelor
	protriptyline	Vivactil
	trimipramine	Surmontil
Monoamine oxidase inhibitors (MAOIs)*	isocarboxazid	Marplan
	phenelzine	Nardil
	tranylcypromine	Parnate

*rarely prescribed for young people because of the strict dietary limitations that MAOIs require

accompany anorexia nervosa (e.g., major depression disorder or anxiety disorder), the fact that these drugs provided at most a "slight" effect is surprising. Some researchers believe that the malnutrition inherent in anorexia nervosa depletes serotonin and might interfere with the therapeutic action of antidepressants, especially SSRIs. In other words, the lower the patient's weight the less effective the drugs will be. Cathleen's son Phil was started on the SSRI paroxetine (Paxil) before he entered an eating disorders clinic, and it had little effect.

"In the long run," she says, "the drug didn't do much for him because his weight was so low when they started him on it. His doctor informed me that because his brain had suffered from the effects of starvation and malnutrition, just like all the other parts of his body, drugs like *"the drug didn't do much* Paxil wouldn't be effective until he *for him because his weight* started gaining weight. Still, he *was so low . . ."* stayed on it until he reached his goal weight and then came off it soon after that. His doctor had no strong feelings about the medication and left it up to Phil and me to decide. Phil really wanted to be off it, so we all agreed he could stop. He had no problems coming off it and everything worked out fine. I'm not sure if the Paxil made a difference, but his attitude changed completely as he began to regain weight."

Apart from antidepressants, atypical antipsychotic drugs, a class of medication usually used to treat severe mental disorders like schizophrenia or bipolar disorder (manic depression), have also been considered as a possible treatment for acute anorexia nervosa because of their association with weight gain. In fact, several case reports have described improvement from the use of olanzapine (Zyprexa) in the treatment of children, adolescents, and adults with anorexia nervosa, making this a potentially promising area for new research.

For bulimia nervosa, virtually every class of antidepressant medication has been studied in trials for adult patients with this disorder, and the evidence is quite clear that antidepressants help patients control their binge eating and purging. It is not clear that any particular medication is the most effective, but in general, SSRIs are better tolerated and have fewer side effects, resulting in their being the first pharmacological treatment of choice for adults with bulimia nervosa. Specifically, the SSRI fluoxetine (Prozac) is the only drug approved by the FDA for the treatment of bulimia nervosa in adults. Results of a trial reported in 2003 suggest that this drug is well tolerated by and may be useful for adolescents with this illness as well. In controlled trials, antidepressant treatment for bulimia nervosa has reduced rates of binge eating and vomiting by sometimes up to 75%, with both depressed and nondepressed patients with bulimia nervosa responding equally well to these drugs. It should be noted, however, that many patients with eating disorders are reluctant to use medication and a significant number end treatment prematurely. Moreover, despite convincing evidence of the effectiveness of this class of medication for the treatment of bulimia nervosa, residual symptoms of the illness persist in many of those treated.

Some new pharmacological agents may hold promise for the development of other medications for this disorder. Both the anti-obesity agent sibutramine (Meridia) and the anticonvulsant topiramate (Topamax) may be beneficial for the treatment of binge eating in adults. The serotonin antagonist ondansetron (Zofran), which is used for the treatment of chemotherapy-induced nausea and vomiting, has also been used to treat adults with an especially stubborn ("refractory") case of bulimia nervosa. However, research on the use of these drugs has not yet been applied to adolescents, and more trials are needed before any conclusions can be drawn as to their effectiveness and safety for younger patients with eating disorders.

That particular point, by now an all too familiar theme to you, also applies to the previously mentioned psychotropic medications that have been tried in adolescents with eating disorders. None of these drugs has been scientifically proven to be effective for this age group, and their pharmacological actions in the still-maturing minds and bodies of teens are not well studied. Some biological factors inherent in adolescents may affect the metabolism and efficacy of psychiatric medications, such as immature neurotransmitter systems in the brain, rapid liver metabolism, and shifting hormonal levels. Certainly, as with all medicines, the patient's response must be monitored so that adjustments can be made if necessary. Shirley's daughter Jody, who was struggling with bulimia nervosa, did not have a good response to medication, but it is possible she might have if she had been more closely observed.

"Jody became depressed and anxious as a result of her binge/purge behaviors, so drugs were prescribed," she says. "She took Paxil for depression as well to reduce the urge to purge. She was also given Ativan for anxiety. Unfortunately, their effectiveness was limited because a physician didn't monitor the dosages. A psychiatrist had prescribed the meds on the recommendation of Jody's psychologist, but there was never any follow-up. In many cases, the prescribed dosage of a drug can make all the difference in how the person responds to it. But because of negative side effects, Jody eventually made the decision to take herself off the drugs. I'll never know what might have happened had the dosages been changed or she'd been prescribed different medications."

Safety must also be a primary consideration when prescribing psychotropic medications for adolescents with eating disorders, especially for those who are medically unstable. TCAs and mood stabilizers, which tend to be less frequently used today than in the past, have potentially serious side effects. In particular, although a clear causal link has not been documented, TCAs have been associated with sudden death among adoles-

Safety must also be a primary consideration when prescribing psychotropic medications for adolescents with eating disorders . . .

cents without eating disorders, and the cardiac abnormalities associated with anorexia nervosa, in theory, could increase the risks of tricyclic use in this group.

In addition, like adults, adolescents with eating disorders are prone to develop other behavioral problems, such as substance use, which may increase the risk of side effects from prescribed psychotropic drugs. In those adolescents who are sexually active, ensuring adequate birth control is also important to prevent the potentially harmful effects of psychotropic medications to the fetus during pregnancy.

Also alarming are the now much-publicized concerns about the potential suicide risk of antidepressant use, especially of SSRIs, in young people. These concerns culminated in October 2004, when the U.S. Food and Drug Administration (FDA) issued a Public Health Advisory about the increased risk of suicidal thoughts and behavior ("suicidality") in children and adolescents being treated with these medications. As part of its report, the agency directed the manufacturers not only of SSRIs but of *all* antidepressant medications to add a "black box" label warning health professionals about the increased risk of suicidality in children and adolescents who are prescribed these medications. This revised labeling is based on studies of five SSRIs—including citalopram (Celexa), fluoxetine (Prozac), fluvoxamine (Luvox), paroxetine (Paxil), and sertraline (Zoloft)—as well as four "atypical" antidepressants—bupropion (Wellbutrin), mirtazapine (Remeron), nefazodone (Serzone), and venlafaxine (Effexor XR). According to the FDA, the action was based on "conclusions about the increased risk of suicidal thoughts and the necessary actions for physicians prescribing these antidepressant drugs and for the children and adolescents taking them." It is important to emphasize, however, that there were no reported cases of suicide during the studies.

FDA Warning

In its October 2004 order that the makers of all antidepressant drugs add stronger warning statements to their product labeling, the FDA determined that the following points are appropriate for inclusion in the warning:

- Antidepressants increase the risk of suicidal thinking and behavior (suicidality) in children and adolescents with major depression and other mental disorders.

- Health care professionals considering the use of an antidepressant in a child or adolescent for any clinical purpose must balance the risk of increased suicidality with the clinical need.

- Patients who are started on therapy should be observed closely for clinical worsening, suicidality, or unusual changes in behavior.

- Families and caregivers should be advised to closely observe the patient and to communicate with the prescriber.

- A statement regarding whether the particular drug is approved for any pediatric indications and, if so, which ones. (Only Prozac has been specifically approved for the treatment of major depression in pediatric patients. Prozac, Zoloft, Luvox, and Anafranil [clomipramine] are approved for treating pediatric obsessive-compulsive disorder.)

The American Academy of Child and Adolescent Psychiatry has provided a useful and detailed review of these issues, which can be found on its Web site, www.aacap.org. Information from the FDA can be seen at www.fda.gov.

What do the FDA's warning and the other potential safety risks or side effects of psychotropic medications mean for you and your child? What should you do if your teen's treatment provider recommends medication? As with any drug, the benefits as well as the risks need to be weighed before initiating treatment. For example, a cancer patient must consider such possible side effects as severe nausea, fatigue, and hair and weight loss before starting chemotherapy. On the other hand, chemotherapy can usually help a patient live for months or even years in remission. Similarly, and as many experts stressed during a hearing that the FDA held a month before issuing its advisory, the potential benefit of antidepressants, especially for a young person who is dangerously depressed, far outweighs the risk. They can, in short, help to save that child's life.

But clearly, the decision to put your own child on medication should be based on a careful consideration of his or her circumstances and state of mind, and it is essential that you play an active role in the decision-making process by discussing with your child's doctor the pros and cons of the medication that might be prescribed. In the course of your discussion, you might ask such questions as

. . . it is essential that you play an active role in the decision-making process . . .

- What are the generic and brand names of the medication?

- What is it supposed to do?

- How soon should we see results?

- When and how often should my teen take the medication?

- How long should my teen stay on the medication?

- Will my teen need to limit any activities while taking the drug?

- Does the medication interact with alcohol, other drugs, or certain foods?

- What are the possible side effects of the medication?

- Which of these side effects are most serious?

Carefully monitoring your child's behavior after a medication has been started is also imperative, not only to ensure that he or she is taking the drug as prescribed but also to watch for certain red flags that may indicate an adverse reaction to its effects. If your child is prescribed an antidepressant, for example, you should immediately notify the doctor if the following symptoms develop or become worse: anxiety, panic attacks, agitation, irritability, hostility, impulsiveness, extreme restlessness, insomnia, self-injurious behavior, and suicidal thoughts.

Relapse Prevention

Relapse is defined as the reappearance of eating-disorder symptoms or the deterioration of a person's condition following an initially successful response to treatment. For example, if your son was treated for anorexia nervosa and his weight was restored, you should suspect a relapse if he starts losing weight again, begins exercising excessively, or avoids family meals. For bulimia nervosa, indications that your daughter might be relapsing following treatment could include self-disparaging remarks about how fat she's gotten or signs that she's binge eating and purging again.

Relapses are indeed common among people with eating disorders, but just how common is debatable. Figures on the actual rates of relapse are imprecise, largely because the research on this subject is not consistent in its use of key terminology to characterize the continuum of experiences—the ups and downs—that may occur between a person's initial treatment and that person's ultimate recovery. Terms like *treatment response, relapse, remission,* and *recovery* tend to be used differently from one scientific study to the next, which makes relapse estimates from different studies difficult to com-

Relapses are indeed common among people with eating disorders . . .

pare. This variation also undermines attempts to establish standardized guidelines for effective relapse prevention, defined as maintenance therapy for individuals who have completed initial treatment and achieved a certain measure of symptomatic recovery.

That said, the following surveys what, on balance, are estimated to be the relapse rates for the two main eating disorder syndromes and describes what is currently known about the types of relapse preventions that have been tried with patients who have these illnesses.

Relapse Rates and Relapse Prevention for Anorexia Nervosa

The majority of patients with anorexia nervosa who are hospitalized due to the severity of their illness respond well to treatment as inpatients. Unfortunately, follow-up studies indicate that the post-hospital period is fraught with difficulty, showing a significant resurgence of symptoms and relapse rates generally ranging between 30% and 50%, with some rates as high as 70%. Moreover, the rates are as significant for adolescents as they are for adults. In a study of 95 patients between the ages of 12 to almost 18 years old, for example, nearly 30% of those who successfully completed their inpatient program relapsed following discharge.

Despite these sobering figures, the findings of at least one study (of post-hospitalized adults) do indicate a positive prospect: that if the weight an individual gains during hospitalization is maintained for a year after discharge, the risk of subsequent weight loss declines dramatically. In other words, the longer a patient can maintain a normal weight after hospitalization, the lower the risk of relapse, so the first few months following discharge are crucial.

The same types of psychological treatments that we described previously are also used to prevent relapses in the post-hospital period for anorexia nervosa. The Maudsley method of family therapy for anorexia nervosa was, in fact, originally designed as a post-hospital treatment, delivered over the course of one year following inpatient care. The findings from the initial study of this method reported that it was more effective than individual supportive therapy for individuals whose age of onset for anorexia nervosa was 18 years or younger and whose illness had a duration of less than three years. Treatment gains in this group were largely maintained at a five-year follow-up assessment, suggesting that changes initiated by family therapy serve to prevent relapses and to enhance the treatment's long-term effectiveness for patients with anorexia nervosa. Although this small study is the only one that has focused on the post-hospital treatment for adolescents with anorexia nervosa, the positive results suggest that the Maudsley method be strongly considered in order to prevent relapse following successful hospital care.

A version of CBT treatment has been designed to treat patients with anorexia nervosa in the year following inpatient treatment. This version focuses on the cognitive and behavioral processes involved in the overvaluation of weight and shape, disordered eating behavior, and low self-esteem thought to be at the core of maintaining the eating disorder. Based on a sample of 33 adults, a recent study demonstrated a significant advantage of CBT over the comparison treatment of nutritional counseling, providing at least preliminary support for the use of CBT as a viable option in preventing relapses and promoting recovery in adults following inpatient hospitalization. However, as yet, there is no evidence regarding the efficacy of CBT for relapse prevention among adolescents with anorexia nervosa.

What about the use of medication in relapse prevention? As noted earlier in this chapter, antidepressants are not effective in treating anorexia nervosa in severely underweight patients, and there is not sufficient information to judge whether they would be of any more help in preventing relapse once weight has been restored.

Relapse Rates and Relapse Prevention for Bulimia Nervosa

Relapse rates for patients with bulimia nervosa are estimated at around 30%. No clinical trials evaluating psychological treatments for acute symptoms of bulimia nervosa have specifically focused on relapse prevention for this disorder; instead, relapse prevention is typically an integrated component of the initial treatment. Most studies suggest that the majority of adults who respond well to initial CBT, the best evidence-based treatment for bulimia nervosa, continue to do well after these interventions have ended, with the most enduring recovery occurring in those people who achieved full remission of binge eating and purging by the end of treatment. But, again, CBT has not been systematically studied in adolescents with bulimia nervosa. Similarly, while the Maudsley method of family therapy appears quite useful both for treating anorexia nervosa and reducing relapse for that disorder, it has only recently been adapted as an initial treatment for bulimia nervosa, so there is no information about its effectiveness in preventing relapse.

There is strong evidence that antidepressant medications are useful in the treatment of adult bulimia nervosa patients, at least in the short term, but how long medication treatment should continue in order to sustain improvement is unclear. Most psychiatrists believe that the rate of relapse is greater when medication is discontinued after only a few months, and recommend that medications be continued for at least six months.

At least one of the parents interviewed for this book expressed a wish that when her daughter relapsed with bulimia nervosa she had been prescribed an antidepressant. "When Linda was hospitalized the first time, the doctors didn't think she was depressed," Kay says. "She was the cheerleader of the ward. That was because she had such a good way of hiding her problems.

> "She was the cheerleader of the ward. That was because she had such a good way of hiding her problems. . . ."

Her friends didn't even know she was bulimic. One time while she was in the hospital, she asked one of the doctors if she could go on antidepressants, and he told her she could if she were hospitalized again. Then, when she was hospitalized again, I asked another doctor on the ward about medication, and she replied that she felt cognitive-behavioral therapy was better. Well, we had been doing that for over a year and here we were again. I wish we'd had the chance to try medication. I know it isn't always the answer and many times the kids won't stay on it, but it would have been nice to think we tried."

Unfortunately, the research is just not available to testify to the effectiveness of medications in preventing relapses in teenagers. The studies that are available have focused only on adults, and it is uncertain whether their results would apply to adolescents or whether using antidepressant medications to prevent relapse in younger patients would involve special considerations relevant to this age group.

What to Do If Your Child Relapses

The bottom line for you as the parent of an adolescent with either bulimia nervosa or anorexia nervosa is vigilance and then preemptive action at the first signs of a relapse. If you have even a slight suspicion that your child is slipping back into disordered eating patterns after an initially successful course of treatment, it is important that you contact his or her treatment provider(s), as relapses can often be more severe than the first occurrence of the disease. As Donna recalls, one summer Chelsey "fell into a deep depression and the anorexia returned. She denied it, of course, but I finally told her she had to go back to the eating disorder clinic. The doctor there was very worried about her health, did an abbreviated assessment, and said she was in critical condition, that she was even sicker than she'd been when she was there the first time. That's why I think it's important for other parents to know what they're in for, which is years of dealing with a seemingly successful recovery followed by relapse."

. . . relapses can often be more severe than the first occurrence of the disease.

Ultimately, as Donna's experience suggests, you may need to hold steady in your resolve to support your child's recovery over the long haul and to work closely with his or her providers throughout the twists and turns the recovery process may take. These illnesses are complex, and even in adults, on whom most of the research has been conducted, they can be frustratingly stubborn to resolve. The same is true for adolescents. But with vigilance and persistence, you'll go a long way toward helping your child overcome the various challenges the eating disorder and its treatment may present.

Navigating the Health Care System

It is a sad fact that the battle against these extremely difficult illnesses is sometimes made worse by the health care system itself.

"When Chelsey went to the doctor," Donna says, "I was told she was in critical condition and needed to be admitted immediately for inpatient treatment. I called our health insurance company to make sure treatment would be covered. When they said no, my husband and I decided we had to admit Chelsey regardless and could fight about the insurance later. I then got a call from the hospital's business office telling me that Chelsey's care would cost $1,600 a day. I again called the insurance company and, after a lot of contentiousness, they finally agreed to pay, but only for three days. The doctor told us the treatment would take much longer, but that without it, Chelsey would die. So my husband told the people at the hospital we'd pay for whatever the insurance didn't cover. After Chelsey was admitted, I was relieved about the fact that she was finally getting treatment. However, the better I felt about her, the angrier I got about our insurance company refusing to pay. So I set out on a campaign to make them pay. It eventually worked somewhat because they finally agreed to pay for seven days of inpatient treatment, but that was it. They refused to pay for more. With Chelsey in treatment for over a month, you can figure out just how much the insurance didn't cover.

"The worst part of it all, besides the exhaustive fighting back and forth almost daily, was that Chelsey thought she was destroying our family because she was so worried about how much her care was costing. What a crime it is to put a person who is sick in that position."

". . . Chelsey thought she was destroying our family because she was so worried about how much her care was costing."

Because eating disorders often require a broad range of treatment for both physical complications and psychological issues, many health insurance providers balk at footing the bill. If a company does cover eating disorders, it usually has very specific (and inadequate) guidelines that limit treatment substantially. Consequently, like Donna, many parents of adolescents with eating disorders find themselves not only helping their child battle a potentially life-threatening disease but also waging war against insurance carriers who nickel-and-dime them about every little bit of treatment their child so desperately needs.

When President Bill Clinton signed the Mental Health Parity Act of 1996, it was viewed as the first step in eliminating discrimination against the mentally ill. Taking effect on January 1, 1998, the landmark law mandated that employers who have more than 50 workers and who offer group health insurance must also provide coverage for mental illness equal to the lifetime and annual caps set for physical ailments. As the Centers for Medicare and Medicaid Services states, "If your health plan has a $1 million lifetime limit on medical and surgical benefits, it cannot put a $100,000 lifetime limit on mental health benefits."

But there's a catch: Although the law mandates "parity" for the treatment of mental illness with regard to dollar limits, it does not require group health plans to offer mental health coverage if their benefits packages don't already do so. Only those group plans that already provide mental health benefits and are sponsored by employers with 50 or more workers are subject to the law. Otherwise, insurers can still charge higher copayments and deductibles and have lower treatment limits for mental health benefits because the law only covers lifetime and annual limits. Additionally, existing state parity laws were not preempted by the federal law, so depending on what state you live in, certain coverage remains in effect, which can, on occasion, exclude certain conditions like eating disorders.

So what does all this mean to you as a parent, and how can you make sure your insurance carrier pays for the treatment your child needs to recover from an eating disorder? On its website, the National Eating Disorders Association (NEDA) posts an entire list of recommendations on how to fight for appropriate and necessary care. That list can be accessed by logging onto www.nationaleatingdisorders.org. Highlights are as follows:

- Get a complete assessment that includes a medical evaluation of your child so as to develop a whole picture of what type of care is needed (e.g., inpatient, outpatient, partial hospitalization).

- As soon as a certain treatment plan has been advised, ask your insurance company or health care provider for recommendations to programs or specialists covered under your plan.

- Should the company representative you speak with tell you your child's needs are not covered under your plan, ask to speak with the medical director of the company. Also talk to your employer or human resources department. Since employers pay part or all of the bills for medical coverage for their entire workforce, they are in a better position to pressure the insurance company into providing needed services.

- Every time you speak to someone at the insurance company, make sure to write down that person's name as well as the date and time of the conversation. If you put any requests for services in writing, make copies of everything before mailing. Such documentation may be necessary for you to prove your efforts to secure payment (e.g., in case your insurance company tells you that they have no record of your phone calls or that your written requests were never received).

- If all of your attempts fail to secure some type of payment from your insurance company, pay for it yourself (as Donna did) and then continue to pursue reimbursement.

Some of the parents whose experiences inform this book lost their children to the consequences of an eating disorder. In Donna's case, that loss was compounded by her insurance company's adamant refusal to provide adequate coverage for the treatment Chelsey needed. "Unlike some people in this country, I've never been 'sue happy,'" says Donna. "But I wanted to send a message to the company that denied my daughter a chance to recover from the deadly disorder that had overwhelmed her. When we were paying our hard-earned money for premiums every month, the company was only too happy to take it. But when it came time for them to pay back, they insisted our coverage was too limited and wouldn't accommodate certain treatments Chelsey desperately needed. That's why I decided to pursue a lawsuit against them." In fact, in some states, legal action by parents has led to substantial changes in how much coverage must be provided by insurance companies.

Valerie's daughter Audra has survived anorexia nervosa, but their experience with insurance providers was no less frustrating. Valerie offers the following advice:

"The best thing I can tell other parents about fighting the system is to write letters or send e-mails to all of your government officials. The longer your child is denied treatment, the greater the chance that the disease will be fatal. It's true that government officials always pass on the requests to someone else, but it's been my experience that most requests eventually do wind up on the desk of someone who will take action. The more letters you send the better, and don't bother to wait for responses. Just keep sending pleas for assistance as fast as you can get them out.

"If your child is on Medicaid, don't give up. You'll inevitably be told that treatment is not covered or that the state doesn't have the money to pay for treatment. I was even told one time that 'anorexia is a weight gain, weight loss disorder and we don't cover that.' If I had been asking for help for a heart condition, kidney failure, or osteoporosis—all of which were symptoms my daughter displayed at the time—she could have received immediate treatment. However, since her primary diagnosis was anorexia, the insurance company did not want to pay for treatment. So you must continue to make calls and write letters until your child is accepted in a treatment program. If everybody keeps at it, maybe one day all those government officials who received letters from grieving parents begging for help will change the laws so that mental illnesses and physical illnesses are treated the same under insurance."

Kay reiterates Valerie's advice:

"Keep pushing your insurance carriers. You will get frustrated, but don't give up on trying to find the right care for your child and don't give up on your child. You never know what combination of treatment will work. It's never the same for any one person and that's why eating disorders are so difficult to treat."

"You will get frustrated, but don't give up . . ."

Chapter Four

Daily Life with the Teen Who Has an Eating Disorder

Helping an adolescent face and then overcome an eating disorder raises some unique challenges for parents, and indeed, for the outer circle of other adults—a teacher or an athletic coach, say—who may play an active role in that teenager's life. This is true both before and after the individual has received treatment for the illness. If your daughter is showing signs of bulimia nervosa, you might be wondering how best to confront her about this possibility. Or you might be worried that your son, who was treated for anorexia nervosa, may be slipping back into patterns you thought were safely in the past, such as obsessing about food and calories, exercising feverishly, or wearing oversized clothes. Or you might be a coach or a teacher who has noticed that your star runner on the school track team is forcing herself to throw up before every race or that your straight-A math student seems listless and is excruciatingly thin.

Adults confronted with the possibility that their child or a child they know might have an eating disorder face many dilemmas: What is the best approach you should take when talking to the teen, and how should you prepare yourself for the conversation? If your child has already been treated for an eating disorder, what can you do to assure progress toward recovery? Also, what support is available for *you* as you try to help a child not only face her disorder or cope with his illness, but also survive and get beyond it? Can teachers, coaches, or other adults in a teen's life assist in this effort and in effect serve as a second line of defense, behind the first line that parents and health care professionals represent, in the fight against these syndromes?

This chapter offers some basic tips for parents and other adults on navigating the difficult waters of everyday life with a child who has an eating disorder, whether that disorder is only suspected or is now confirmed. These recommendations summarize information given in some of the resources listed at the end of this book, but they also draw on the personal experiences of parents themselves and on the practical wisdom they've gleaned from facing these disorders in their own children. Varied as their experiences are, they all speak to a single reality: that you can and do have a very important role to play in helping a teenager beat an eating disorder, whether you're the parent of that teen or another adult with a direct connection to that child's daily life.

. . . you can and do have a very important role to play in helping a teenager beat an eating disorder . . .

The advice in this chapter is by no means intended as a substitute for professional treatment. This is especially true in the event of a medical emergency. If a teenager you know is showing major indications of having an eating disorder (e.g., extreme weight loss, dizziness or blackouts, profound depression) or is a suicide risk, it is imperative that you not take time to debate with that child about the need to get help. You must take action and get professional attention for the child imme-

diately. As we emphasized in Chapter 2, the medical consequences of eating disorders or of their possible concurrent conditions are severe and potentially fatal, and the sooner an
adolescent begins treatment, the better his or her chances are
of recovery. The tips in this chapter may help you to avert such
an emergency in the first place or to handle the aftermath of a
crisis if one in fact does occur, but they are not stand-ins for
medical advice or treatment. Those can come only from a qualified professional.

Getting the Teen to Treatment:
Communication and Persistence

Talking to adolescents can be difficult under the best of circumstances. Due to physical and psychological changes, academic stress, and peer pressure, formerly outgoing kids can grow
moody and withdrawn, preferring to shut themselves off from
family and friends and to opt out of activities they previously
enjoyed. The challenges of contemporary family life can further complicate things. One parent going off to work while the
other stays home to tend to family affairs is now the exception
rather than the rule in our society. In most households nowa-
days, both parents work, often for very long hours, in order to
support their family. And many households are headed by single
parents, who must cope with working all week while also maintaining the home and tending to their kids' needs. These demands can take a toll on the ability of family members to stay
in touch with each other.

Communicating with teenagers about something as stigma-
tizing as their anorexic or bulimic behavior can be all the more
difficult because of the secrecy and shame that accompany these

Talking: It's a Good Thing

"Communication was definitely a problem at our house before Vanessa was diagnosed with anorexia nervosa," says Susan. "Both my husband and I worked and had three busy kids who were always on the go. There never seemed to be time to sit down for family meals. Everybody was into his or her own life and, if we did talk, it was usually while standing around the kitchen eating something on the run. In hindsight, I would make more time for family life and coordinate at least a few family meals. Some kids are likely to resent this at first, but it's important to come together as a family, even if it's only once or twice a week. It gives your kids the message that you care and gives *you* a chance to stop, sit back, and really listen to them."

disorders. So while it is important to talk to your child as soon as you see certain signs and symptoms of an eating disorder appear, it is equally important to do so thoughtfully, calmly, and with advanced preparation. Suspect that your daughter is bulimic? Charging in and yelling things like, "I know you're making yourself throw up and you've got to stop it right now!" will serve no purpose other than to make her react defensively or withdraw from you altogether. It's also likely that she, like many individuals with eating disorders, may be in such denial about her condition that she can't yet acknowledge to herself that her behavior is harmful. Your yelling at her or angrily asserting your authority won't bring her out of that defensive stance. But staying grounded, thinking things through, and planning ahead before you broach the topic with your child will help both you and her to talk about the situation openly and candidly.

Preparing Your Approach

One of the first things to do prior to approaching a teenager about his or her eating-disorder symptoms is to learn about the illness itself, as well as about weight, exercise, and nutrition. Individuals with eating disorders tend to have skewed ideas about these subjects and are likely to make excuses for their behavior. Arming yourself with information from valid sources will help you to dispel the kind of responses you might get from your son or daughter, such as "I read a magazine article that said I weigh more than I should for how tall I am," or "I eat as many calories as I need to. I know because I looked it up."

Some parents have actually brought pamphlets, books, and articles to the initial discussion with their children. These can be helpful, but you need to be very careful about the material you ultimately choose. "My first introduction to eating disorders, besides the death of Karen Carpenter," Jody's mother Shirley explains, "came with the reading of an article that appeared in a local newspaper during Jody's first semester at college. With graphic detail, the woman described her journey into bulimic behaviors. It appeared that she began with the same behaviors I had witnessed in Jody: excessive exercise, counting calories, weighing herself constantly. This was my first reading on bulimia and it scared me."

Shirley immediately sent the article to Jody with "a gentle letter" explaining her concerns. Jody initially replied that Shirley worried needlessly, but later she revealed that the article had actually given her a lot of "how-to's" on bulimia. "I hadn't noticed the many details on specific behaviors the article described," Shirley states. "But they were all Jody had noticed."

The fact is that many articles and books, particularly memoirs written by those who have had anorexia nervosa or bulimia nervosa, tend to be brutally honest about behaviors like purging or laxative abuse. Rather than serving as warnings of the dangers of eating disorders, these descriptions can provide at-risk teens or those who already have eating disorders with provocative tips about dieting and weight loss practices that they haven't yet tried.

If you do consider bringing reading material to your child's attention, we recommend pamphlets and brochures that have been produced by national eating disorder associations or mental health associations: They purposely avoid describing anything other than signs and symptoms and don't elaborate on behaviors that at-risk teens might be tempted to imitate. Consult your pediatrician, family doctor, a school counselor, or a mental health association about appropriate literature that they might recommend. There are also numerous national organizations that have Web sites with information about the signs and symptoms of eating disorders, which you could print out and share with your child. These sites are listed in the Resources section of this book.

Before approaching your child, also do some research on what local resources and treatment options are available to you and your teen. Again, a professional should be able to provide information and referrals for specialists in your area. They may also be able to help you find support groups for parents of children with eating disorders. Additionally, the Harvard Eating Disorder Center (HEDC) suggests that parents initially meet with a referred therapist before talking to their child so as to allow any expressions of strong emotions or anger to be worked out in advance. If this is not a possibility for you because of time or financial constraints, using a relative or trusted friend as a sounding board might help. They won't be in the position to offer professional advice, but you'll still have an opportunity to vent your frustrations at them rather than at your teen.

Once you're prepared to meet with your son or daughter, pick a place that's comfortable and familiar—the living room, the child's bedroom, your den—and make sure you allow as much time as you need to talk about the issue thoroughly. This is a tough task you're undertaking. Broaching the subject while driving your teen to school or starting the conversation when there is the likelihood you'll be interrupted will only delay what you hope to accomplish. Make sure also that your first discussion is private: The only people present should be you, your spouse or partner, and your teenager. Siblings, grandparents, aunts, uncles, cousins, or friends should not be included, as their presence could cause your child to feel under attack or ganged up on, thereby distracting him or her from what you're saying.

Make sure also that your first discussion is private.

The Conversation

When initiating the discussion, first stress how much you love your child and that your concerns stem from that love. It sounds trite, but all teenagers, no matter how grown up they seem, do need to hear this reassurance from you—that you have only their best interests at heart and are not the enemy. Be straightforward and direct about what's bothering you about your child's behavior. Try to remain as calm as possible. The attitude you'd like to convey is that you are concerned, but not panicked, and that as a parent who loves your child, you are committed to figuring out what is wrong and helping to get it taken care of.

Even though you and your daughter or son might have been very close prior to the development of the eating disorder, it is important for you to be steadfast in your parental role. As Shirley points out, "Jody and I had always been very close. Therefore, I attempted a friendly rather than firm approach, assuming it would make it easier for her to listen and comprehend my heart-to-heart chat. Unfortunately, I didn't realize how involved and distracted her brain was. I thought she was capable of being rational. That was an erroneous assumption on my part. Jody needed a parent, not a friend." Being a parent to your child means you can be authoritative but not dictatorial. You can still be gentle and compassionate while remaining firm in your effort to convince your child that he or she needs your help.

During your discussion, refrain from using such negative phrases as "You're too skinny," or "Can't you see what you're doing to yourself?" Such an approach can backfire. "I kept thinking that if I could get her to see what she was doing to herself," says one mother whose daughter developed anorexia nervosa, "she'd be able to figure it out and stop losing weight. But I was wrong. Following a heated confrontation that dissolved into a screaming match, I finally dragged her to a full-length mirror and forced her to look at herself. She was horrified, but not for the same reason I was. What I thought she'd see was the walking skeleton she'd become. However, what she saw was 'a huge, hideous, grotesque, inhuman freak.' Of course, she couldn't explain this to me until after she'd started therapy and her description still haunts me. She's such a beautiful child, and I am still trying to understand why she saw herself as something so horrifying. And even though she's been on the road to recovery for a couple of years now, I wake up every morning praying she'll never have to see herself that way again."

"A huge, hideous, grotesque, inhuman freak"—this is a typical self-image that individuals in the grip of an eating disorder have. Assume that your daughter, based on the behavior you've observed in her recently, sees herself in much the same way. Do not assume that your son, just because he's a boy, is somehow able to see himself in a better light. He can't at this time see himself as you do, and so try to reach him—to open up a dialogue with him—through personal observations that don't directly challenge this self-image *per se* but that may help him understand why you're worried. Statements such as "I've noticed that you seem very anxious lately," or "I hear you say you're too fat and that worries me" don't assign blame but instead put the emphasis on you and on what you're feeling about the situation.

If your child's initial response is anger or denial, try to stay cool and keep your own emotions in check. If you become angry, it will only convince her that you are indeed the enemy—that you're someone who wants to take away the only effective method she thinks she has for dealing with food and weight. Also, since much shame accompanies eating disorders, your child may be furious with you for exposing her "secret." By remaining calm, you stand a better chance of getting her to eventually hear your concerns.

If you become angry, it will only convince her that you are indeed the enemy . . .

On the other hand, some children may use an opposite tactic in an attempt to placate you. Instead of blowing up, they might remain completely cool and try to manipulate the conversation so as to take the focus off of them. They could say, "Oh, Mom, you always worry too much. I'm fine, really. Actually, I'm worried about *you*. You work too hard. You need to relax. Why don't you go do that right now? I can take care of myself." A good response to that ploy would be to say that, while you'll be very pleased if they are indeed fine, you still want them to go to the doctor, just to be sure.

Whatever the tone of his or her response, your child is likely to resist your initial attempts at offering help. It's true that some children are actually relieved when their parents offer assistance because it means they no longer have to struggle with their eating disorder by themselves, but they are an exception. Most teens, including those who may even be aware they have an eating disorder, rarely want help; they usually imagine that treatment is all about being forced to get fat. You may, in short, need to talk to your child numerous times—patiently but firmly and authoritatively—before he or she begins to accept the notion of getting help.

And you may have to constantly shore up this acceptance once it comes. It may be tentative or short-lived, and you'll likely have to shift between pushing your son or daughter forward to the next step or pulling back and trying to allow the child's own resolve to develop. The HEDC recommends, for example, that parents not overwhelm their children "with details about a treatment plan" until the teens can first adjust to the sense of shame they may feel now that their illness is no longer a "secret." Once they've adjusted to this difficult "exposure," they might then be comforted by their parents' effort to find help for them.

Still other teenagers might start out amenable to treatment and then suddenly refuse to go. Their excuse could be that they've decided they don't need a doctor and can stop the disordered eating behavior on their own or that they already *have* stopped. Don't buy these excuses. If you believe your child's behavior continues to show the signs and symptoms of an eating disorder, keep talking, keep pressing your points, but if need be, it goes without saying, take action and get your child into treatment immediately.

The Role of Teachers and Coaches: Communicating with a Student or Athlete Who Has an Eating Disorder

Adolescents spend much of their daily lives in school, under the supervision of adults other than their parents, and they can be enormously influenced by anything an authority figure in school says or does. This may be especially true for adolescents at risk of developing eating disorders. Given their tendency to be perfectionistic, they can be deeply affected by what a respected teacher or coach says to them. Whether in the realm of track, basketball, soccer, swimming, dance, drama, or some other activity, negative comments from a coach or a teacher about weight and size can make such a strong impression on adolescent athletes or performers that they may think the only way they can stay on a team or in a class is if they become thinner.

They might even believe they're doing the team or class a favor by becoming smaller. Cathleen's son Phil was on the track team when he started losing a great deal of weight. She worried about him because he seemed "so stressed out" and finally talked to him about the weight loss. His excuse was that he was thinning down to help the team. He told Cathleen that he was so much faster since he'd lost weight. "Just think how much faster I'll be when I've lost even more," he said.

> *They might even believe they're doing the team or class a favor by becoming smaller.*

The desire to excel and to win can be natural, but when overcharged in an impressionable adolescent, it can lead to damaging results. Books like Joan Ryan's *Little Girls in Pretty Boxes* (1995) describe how the extreme dieting practices of elite athletes such as gymnasts and figure skaters were once encouraged by coaches and teachers. Some Olympic trainers held such unhealthy sway over the lives of young athletes because their methods produced what every country demanded: winners. In other sports as well, some coaches communicated (either verbally or by implication) that the thinner an athlete was, the better shot he or she had at making the team. Similar encouragement for potentially extreme weight loss has also been described in the dance world; the only way for a ballerina to be "in" with a company was to be thin, and dancers even shared tips with each other about how to fast and about the best ways to purge.

Most teachers and coaches now realize the importance of putting more emphasis on health and nutrition rather than on body size. Communicating such values to young athletes can help them stay healthy and active in both the short and long term. In addition, a coach or instructor who doesn't attach a stigma to weight can do a lot to raise an adolescent's self-esteem. Candy, who is now an adult but who as a teenager struggled with binge eating that led to obesity, talks about how her high-school P.E. teacher helped her:

"I started getting really fat when I hit puberty. By the time I turned fifteen, I weighed 200 pounds. There were a lot of problems at home, I was really depressed, and kept eating everything in sight. But I also loved sports and my ninth-grade Phys Ed teacher was terrific. First, she made me a part of the team that was entered in a local gymnastics exhibition. I remember thinking 'Is she out of her mind?' because I knew I'd be the fattest girl there and would surely cause us to lose. Well, we didn't win, but I did the best double rolls of anybody thanks to her. She also put me on our school's relay track team that was entered in an all-city tournament. All the other teams looked so smug when I lined up because I'm sure they thought 'That fat girl can't beat us,' but we actually won the meet. And then, to everybody's shock, Mrs. Morrison made me first string on the basketball team. We wound up winning another all-city tournament, and I received an award for having the highest rebound total. While it took me years to learn what my overeating meant and to then get myself down to a healthy weight, I'm still grateful to Mrs. Morrison for seeing me as the person I was rather than just another fat kid she had to deal with. Attitude is everything and hers changed my life."

Providing positive reinforcement can certainly help an at-risk adolescent, but teachers and coaches who suspect that a student or a team member of theirs has an eating disorder can help in other ways as well. The following recommendations are offered by the Harvard Eating Disorders Center and the National Eating Disorders Association. Teachers and coaches can

- Talk directly to the student, making sure they're prepared before starting the discussion by learning as much as they can about eating disorders and about what relevant resources might be available to the student at the school or in the community. They should also find out about school policy regarding students with eating disorders and how it might affect his or her participation in classes and sports.

- Use a quiet, private place for their conversation with the student so that his or her confidentiality is maintained, and allow enough time for the talk to occur without interruption.

- Share their concerns in a manner that conveys personal regard for the teen as a unique individual rather than as just somebody else in class or on the team and that are cast as observations rather than as judgments: for example, "You don't seem to be enjoying class as much as you used to," or "I'm worried that you might be doing more harm than good with those extra-long workouts."

- Anticipate the likelihood that the student may deny he or she has a problem, but avoid a battle of wills likely to upset the student. If things get too heated, it's best to end the conversation and try approaching the student again later.

- Have some resources and referrals available to give to the student in the event he or she accepts the need for help.

- Seek professional help immediately if the student is in a life-threatening situation (i.e., is passing out in class or seems suicidal or depressed).

In addition, teachers, coaches, and other school personnel must maintain meaningful communication not only with each other about a student's behavior at school but most especially with the student's parents. As Bobbie, whose daughter was diagnosed with anorexia nervosa, states:

"My daughter Sarah was throwing away the lunches I made for her every day to take to school because, as she told me later, after she was in treatment, she knew she couldn't be the smartest or the prettiest, but at least wanted to try to be the smallest. But because she wasn't eating, she eventually passed out in chorus class and was sent to the school nurse, who did nothing more than accept her excuse about why she'd fainted ('It was so hot in that room and I was standing on a riser'). Well, I had no idea my kid had passed out in school because nobody told me— not the teacher, not the nurse, nobody. Why one of them didn't call me or talk to me, I'll never know, but it's obvious they weren't talking to each other either. That's why I think schools need to set protocols. Each person, whether it's a teacher, school nurse, counselor, or principal, all need to bring a piece of the puzzle to complete the whole picture that parents can't fill in by themselves."

"I had no idea my kid had passed out in school because nobody told me—not the teacher, not the nurse, nobody."

Treatment and Recovery: Staying the Course, Staying Strong, Staying in Touch

Entering and sticking with a treatment program for a serious illness, including an eating disorder, can be a daunting prospect for anyone. It can be especially so for an adolescent. Some teens can be frightened at the thought of being turned over to strangers, especially if hospitalization is required. Therefore, it is very important for you as a parent to reassure your daughter or son of your continuing emotional support during the treatment process. Knowing of your enduring support can make a big difference in your child's attitude about spending time away from home (if hospitalized) or about outpatient therapy.

It is also important to let the treatment run its course, even if you see your child making good progress early on, and to seek the judgment of his or her doctor or therapist as to when treatment can conclude. Your resolve may sometimes be heart-wrenchingly difficult to sustain: "The greatest strain of visiting her," says Valerie, whose daughter Audra was hospitalized for anorexia nervosa, "wasn't the eight-hour car trip it took to get there, but having to be strong when she begged and pleaded with us to take her home." Your ultimate commitment is to your son's or daughter's long-term recovery and health, not to their assurances that they've recovered or even to intermediate marks of progress that you yourself see. Talk with your child's treatment provider routinely about those marks and assess their significance together and in light of the provider's expertise.

For many teenagers, the battle to overcome an eating disorder can remain a struggle even after a course of treatment. It can be equally stressful for parents, relatives, friends, and other people in the teen's life. The following story is an extreme example of the many ups and downs one parent experienced with her daughter.

Diane's Story

After the diagnosis of anorexia nervosa was established, Diane's daughter Megan started seeing a therapist who specialized in eating disorders. According to Diane, the therapy helped "somewhat," but Megan continued to lose weight and became suicidal.

"She took over-the-counter medications like Benadryl and Tylenol PM by the handful to try to kill herself, then she'd sit in our family therapy sessions and smile smugly, telling us she was fine. We knew she wasn't and finally had to hospitalize her." After a few months, Diane eventually secured a spot for Megan in an eating disorders unit and, once there, her daughter became a model patient. The unit was far away, but Diane drove there to visit her every day while her husband and Megan's younger sister remained at home. After only two weeks, Megan told Diane she was cured and "good to go."

"That was the beginning of two years of hell," Diane says. "When she got home, she went right back to her old habits of not eating, losing weight, and overdosing on pills. Her problems became the focus of my entire life. It was just so weird because, before the eating disorder, Megan was the absolute best kid. She got along great with her little sister, she never got into any trouble, she excelled academically, had lots of friends, and was invited to become a member of any club she wanted to join. Then, practically within the blink of an eye, everything changed and Megan became someone I couldn't even recognize. I kept asking myself how I could've let it happen. I kept thinking that somehow I'd failed as a person and, most importantly, as a mom."

> "Her problems became the focus of my entire life."

With erratic behavior, tremendous mood swings, and more suicide attempts, Megan dictated the household, particularly around food issues.

"She was always telling us what we could and couldn't eat and if we bought something she didn't want us to have, she'd throw it out in the middle of the night. Nights were when her demons came out and that made it very hard for the rest of us. We'd get up in the morning never knowing what we'd find.

One morning was particularly frightening. I walked into her bedroom to wake her up and found it completely destroyed. She had scrawled 'I hate myself' all over the walls and for the first time, I really felt all of her hatred, anger, and pain. I was terrified and searched for her everywhere. I finally found her down in the basement. She was asleep. When I woke her, she just smiled up at me and said, 'Hi, Mom. Guess you could tell I had a bad night, huh?'"

As much as Diane empathized with her daughter, she could also see how much Megan's out-of-control behavior was affecting the family and, in particular, her younger sister.

"We finally came to the conclusion that there was no other choice but to try some tough love. We tried to do it as firmly as possible to let her know we weren't going to back down. We'd already given in to her too many times and it obviously hadn't helped at all. We told her we desperately needed to restore order in the household by setting up some rules. We left it up to her to either conform to our terms or leave. She chose to leave, which broke our hearts, but we had to stand by what we'd said." Megan wound up moving in with her friend Brenda, but was kicked out shortly after she arrived.

"We finally came to conclusion that there was no other choice but to try some tough love. . . ."

"I got a call from Brenda's mother, who told me that Megan's mood swings and wild behavior were distracting Brenda, who was a scholarship student and had to keep her grades up. Also, although I hadn't known it at the time, Megan had started binge eating and was eating Brenda out of house and home. I had to call Megan and tell her that since another family was now involved, she needed to either go back to the hospital or come home. She refused, saying she'd met a boy and would move in with him. That didn't last long either because she wound up in an intensive care unit after overdosing on a combination of prescription antidepressants and sleeping pills. When we arrived at the hospital, she was strapped to her bed and on life support."

Fortunately, Megan survived this crisis and in time she did turn a corner to accept the fact that she needed help. "I'm still trying to put all the pieces of the puzzle together and understand what turned things around for her," Diane says, "and there's still a lot of work to be done, but we're getting there." Megan continues to struggle with the effects of her eating disorder on a daily basis. She is still underweight, has chronic stomach problems, and has trouble moving her bowels because of laxative abuse.

"But the upside," Diane says, "is Megan has started to embrace life again. She eventually wants to finish college and become a nutritionist so she can help other people with eating disorders. If she completes her education and eventually does that, I'll be thrilled, but for right now, I'm just grateful she is alive."

Managing Daily Life

There are no "quick fixes" for eating disorders. As the previous story indicates, recovering from them may take a long time and many patients relapse more than once after their initial treatment. Indeed, more research is needed not only on the causes of eating disorders but also on the triggering events or coexisting conditions that can plunge someone in recovery back into disordered eating habits. Nevertheless, there are many things that parents can do to help their children on a day-to-day basis. As Vanessa's mother Susan says, "We as parents are powerless to 'fix' our children, but we're not powerless in the choices we make to try to help them."

The first step is to recognize that your child's hospitalization or outpatient treatment was a beginning, not an end in itself. Your child has not been "cured" of the disorder, but has simply become strong enough because of initial treatment to at least begin navigating daily life again at home and school. The second step is to recognize that the child's recovery can be especially difficult during this reentry period and will require as much vigilance, patience, and assistance from everyone—family, teachers, coaches, and so on—as when the problem was first recognized.

TIPS AT HOME

The havoc that an eating disorder can wreak not only on affected adolescents but also on their families cannot be overstated. If that has been the case for your family, it may be helpful to convene a meeting of sorts—in short, talk to each other, both individually and as a family, about what has happened in your shared lives. Doing so will help reestablish family connections and defuse tensions, for the teenager with the disorder as well as for everyone else involved. Siblings can be deeply affected by a sister's or a brother's behavior, for example, and they may feel forgotten or abandoned because you've had to focus so much on the child with the illness. If so, try to reassure them that every member of the household is equally important and encourage them to express their feelings.

Siblings . . . may feel forgotten or abandoned because you've had to focus so much on the child with the illness.

As Diane's story illustrates, limits need to be set within the family framework for a teen who has either just returned home from the hospital or is being treated as an outpatient. Avoiding all discussions and confrontations for fear of precipitating a relapse may actually allow her the freedom of falling back into old eating-disordered habits. Conversely, you shouldn't feel you have to constantly police your child. Striking a balance between allowing your teen independence and setting limits on her behavior is the ideal situation, but also a fine line to tread. If you have a problem with how to respond to your child's needs and behavior, talk to her therapist or treatment team for suggestions about the best approaches you can take with her and about how to set limits on behavior that is likely to disrupt the entire household.

Aspects of daily family life and the way in which family members interact with each other will likely need adjustment as well. Take, for example, mealtimes. These of course can be extremely stressful for teens recovering from an eating disorder. They may have become so obsessed with counting calories and carbohydrates and fat grams that even a single bite of food still terrifies them. They are also very aware that everybody in the family knows they have "food issues" and is undoubtedly watching to see what they eat. For that reason, it's best to keep family mealtimes as relaxed as possible. The Center for Young Women's Health (CYWH)—Children's Hospital in Boston recommends, for example, that instead of focusing on food during mealtimes, families should discuss neutral topics like current events, movies, or even the weather to help ease tensions for everyone at the table, including the teen.

Planning meals in advance can also help reduce mealtime stress. Those in the throes of an eating disorder like anorexia nervosa systematically eliminate foods from their diets until they are only eating things that are extremely low in calories, fat, and nutritional value (e.g., lettuce, celery, carrots). During recovery, there-

Planning meals in advance can also help reduce mealtime stress.

fore, it is important to help them expand their list of "safe foods." As part of meal planning, the CYWH suggests that you and your child go grocery shopping together and set a goal of buying one new food to try each week or every other week. If your child is undergoing nutrition counseling, ask the nutritionist's advice about which new foods might be good additions to your menu. If a nutritionist is not available, discuss the subject with your family doctor or even a teacher at school who knows about nutrition.

Cooking and trying out new recipes together are other ways of making food issues less stressful. Do not, however, allow the teen to shop or cook for the family by him- or herself. Many people with eating disorders will feed their families as a way to avoid feeding themselves. By cooking, serving, and then not eating the food they've prepared, they are proving that they are in control of it rather than it controlling them. The meals they serve can often be elaborate and take all day for them to prepare. They may also make a point of serving all the favorite foods they used to eat and of then watching vicariously as their family eats them. If asked why they're not joining the family for such a scrumptious meal, they may say that they did a lot of tasting while making the dish or that they ate a big helping before bringing it to the table. If you and your child cook the meal together, you will be able to observe how much he or she actually does eat before everybody sits down to the table.

The physical changes, such as weight gain, that are brought about by treatment can also cause stress. Those with eating disorders are deathly afraid of being fat. Even if they're in recovery, it still takes a long time for them to come to grips with the return to a healthier lifestyle. Therefore, it's wise to avoid saying things like "You look so much better since you put on weight," or "I'm so proud of you for putting on a few pounds." Such comments, while well-meaning, might cause them to panic because they think, "Oh my god, if they keep making me eat, I'm going to be a blimp! I've got to start losing weight again right now!" Instead, comment positively on changes you've noticed in your child as a person rather than in his or her physical appearance.

At the same time, teenagers in recovery from eating disorders may feel overwhelmed or suffocated by all the attention, at home or in individual and family therapy sessions, that's focused on them, their eating habits, and their interpersonal relationships. You should be sure to give your child a breather from this attention and do things together that don't revolve around food or weight issues. Invite your son to go to a movie with you, or check out the latest exhibition at a local museum with your daughter. Or just window-shop. If the doctor certifies that your child is physically strong enough, you might even suggest a day trip to a favorite getaway spot. As he or she continues to recover, talk to the child's treatment team about scheduling more activities for just the two of you or with the entire family. These will help you to develop and maintain a relationship with your child that is not focused on his or her having an eating disorder.

Earlier in this discussion, Susan spoke of the fact that parents can do a lot to assist their children's recovery from an eating disorder. They can indeed, and so can whole families. As the foregoing suggests, that help can come in the form of changing family life so that it adequately supports the child's treatment and recovery process. The process will likely have some rocky moments along the way, but one of the signs it's going well is when you begin to see your child help him- or herself in truly positive ways. Susan again:

"Before the eating disorder, Vanessa was always the peace-maker in the family. Whenever there was a conflict, she'd step in and calm everybody down. It was a great gift, but when I look back on it, I wonder just how much of herself she was suppressing to keep peace in our home. Since entering therapy, however, she has become much more assertive and now fights with her brother and sister the way most siblings do. Most people with eating disorders use the fact that they're not eating to tell you there's something wrong. They're also in such deep denial that they really don't want to listen to anything you have to say. The fact that she's finally able to talk to everyone and advocate for herself is wonderful."

TIPS AT SCHOOL

Returning to school after a hospitalization can be enormously difficult for adolescents with an eating disorder. They may wonder what their peers know about their absence, or they may worry that they've been a subject of gossip. How they choose to navigate their return—for example, how they respond to questions and concerns about why they were gone or what made them sick—is entirely up to them. Likely they'll be torn about what to do or say. If they choose to share their dilemma with you, you can help by listening and, if you feel it's appropriate, by offering some suggestions. However, if they don't ask for your help or reject your suggestions, don't force the issue or push your point by saying something like "Well, I think you'd feel better if you told so-and-so. After all, you were best friends before all this happened." Some teens might be more comfortable talking to a trusted teacher, coach, or counselor with both knowledge of the eating disorder and enough savvy about the teens' particular peer group to be a good sounding board or to offer good advice.

And some teens decide on their own what they do and don't want others to know, and take reentry into school life as it comes. "When my son Phil was hospitalized, his friends, teachers, and coach were awesome," says Cathleen. "They were so supportive of him just getting well. However, he did not want anyone to know he had an eating disorder and I do think if his friends knew he had anorexia nervosa, they may have treated him differently. It was interesting because, after being out of school for four months, during his second week back, one of his friends asked him, 'What was wrong with you?' Phil told him that life had just gotten to be too much for him, that he was really stressed out, and lost a lot of weight. His friend said, 'Oh, that happened to me, too, but my grades just went down.' How great is that? So simple, yet so complicated."

Still, a student returning to the classroom after hospitalization does present certain challenges, such that reentry can be made easier if you forge a partnership with school personnel and teachers and then routinely stay in touch with them about your child's progress. Some teachers may worry that they have to treat the teen differently from the rest of the class. As the teen's parent, you should urge them to avoid paying undue attention that can embarrass your child—who's already self-conscious enough after all—or that may send the wrong message: that thinness begets greater attention. At the same time, because hospitalization or even outpatient treatment can cause some adolescents with eating disorders to fall behind the rest of the class, a teacher might be tempted to assign extra work so that they can catch up. Even if the teen requests extra work—and this is possible, given that most adolescents with eating disorders tend to be overachievers who pride themselves on succeeding academically—an accelerated program may not be a good solution. The effects of eating disorders can be severe and recovery from them takes time. Since the adolescent's energy and concentration may not yet have returned to the same levels they once were, he or she could be overwhelmed by the pressure of completing more than the regular workload. Instead, you should urge your teen's teachers to focus on how far along he or she is in the course material rather than on where the entire class is and to work with you and your child's treatment team to develop a reasonable, well-paced plan for helping him or her to eventually achieve academic goals.

Adolescents in recovery from an eating disorder may have a special meal plan that requires nutritious snacks. Here, too, you should work with the school to ensure that your child is given the time to take these, but also to be aware of signs that your teen may be relapsing, such as suddenly eating lots of junk food or bolting for the bathroom after lunch.

Phil's mother Cathleen emphasizes the critical importance of this communication between school personnel and families: "I think it's key to watch for anything our children seem to be struggling with, whether it's eating, drinking, drugs, or whatever else might be bothering them. They are all part of our society and have problems coping just like adults. The goal is to raise a healthy, happy, self-confident child. Anything that gets in the way of that is a problem you have to deal with, and deal with it as soon as you possibly can, because the longer it goes on,

> "The goal is to raise a healthy, happy, self-confident child."

the harder it is to change. This can only come by communicating with your child as well as the people they spend time with. I think that catching Phil's problem early made all the difference in how well he's recovered. He's doing so great that it almost seems like a lifetime ago when he was hospitalized and trying to tear the IV out of his arm. He is now one of the top runners on his team and I am so proud of him. His coach has been very supportive, has kept an eye on him all season, and has also made a point of incorporating eating plans into his program, not just for Phil but for all the boys. It's so great because everybody involved wants to make sure Phil stays strong and healthy and, by checking in with each other, we seem to be doing that."

Finding Support from Other Parents

All of the parents who were interviewed for this book expressed the need for support from other parents who were dealing with or had dealt with similar situations. As Megan's mother Diane said, "The greatest help is support from other families. It's absolutely crucial. Eating disorders are family diseases. From Sunday mealtime to every other part of daily life, it all changes and families need to know that they're not alone."

Eating disorders are family diseases.

Indeed, families with the same experiences you're facing now can be a source not only of emotional support but also of practical tips and other information that can help you cope with your child's disorder. The problem is that finding such support locally, which is ideal, might not be easy. "In 1999, I couldn't find any other parents nearby to talk to," says Chelsey's mother Donna. "The doctors couldn't help me, and it was so frustrating. There weren't the number of Web sites about eating disorders that there are now. Mostly I wound up doing a lot of reading, which helped, but I really craved having a one-on-one conversation with somebody who was going through what I was or who had been through it. Even just a little understanding can go a long way to help someone who feels overwhelmed by their situation."

Due to issues of privacy and confidentiality, doctors are re-stricted in the kind of information they can and can't share about their patients. They might be able to obtain another parent's consent so that you can talk to him or her, but your best bet is to try to find an existing support group for parents of children with eating disorders. When Diane eventually did locate one in her area, she was very relieved.

"The first time I went it was so great," she says. "The people there were totally supportive and I was able to share things with them that I couldn't talk to other people about. But I also found it frustrating because it only met once a month. I really wanted to be there more often, just to keep myself grounded."

Then, too, there was an unexpected problem when Megan found out Diane was going to the group. "She became furious with me for talking about her to strangers and screamed at me, 'This isn't your stuff, this is *my* stuff!' I was so taken aback by her anger that I was tempted to tell her I wouldn't go anymore. She was in such a fragile state—both physically and emotionally—and I didn't want to risk upsetting her further. Then I realized that if I didn't do a few things to take care of myself, I'd be no use to her anyway. I'd be letting the disease control me the same way it was controlling Megan, so I finally told her, 'Look, this isn't just about you anymore. Those of us who care about you are involved, too. If you want to stay mad at me, fine, go right ahead, but right now I need help, too.'"

If, after exhausting all local channels, you're still unable to connect with other parents in your area, you might consider starting a support group yourself. That prospect may seem daunting at first, especially if you're trying to juggle work re-sponsibilities, home life, therapy sessions, or hospital visits. If so, think about asking a family member or friend to lend a hand. Lots of people who care about you and your family would probably feel pleased you asked and would be eager to help. They could even assist you in solving some logistical problems, such as where to hold your meetings, and go with you to check out the possibilities. Local businesses, schools, churches, or other organizations might be willing to allow you to use their space or offer to put the word out about your group. Another way to reach potential group members is to place a classified ad in a local publication. There are numerous free newspapers and magazines that are distributed in neighborhoods around the country, and most of them have "Community Events" sections where people can place ads for free (or a nominal fee) if you're not charging admission for your event. You could also print up support-group meeting fliers and post them anywhere you're allowed to, such as in libraries, laundromats, supermarkets, bookstores, or on telephone poles.

Many colleges and universities also have programs on eating disorders. If there is a campus nearby, talk to an administrator or instructor there about making contact with other parents or ask about any support services they offer.

If all else fails, contact the numerous organizations around the country for information, support services, and professional referrals. Their names, phone numbers, and addresses are listed in the Resources section of this book.

Chapter Five

Preventing Eating Disorders

P arents have reason to be optimistic about the outcome of a
child with an eating disorder: Most adolescents with anorexia nervosa or bulimia nervosa do in fact recover. However,
the treatments currently available are not as effective or rapid
as parents and professionals would like, and some youngsters
suffer for a long time. It is critically important that the search
continue for more precise and useful definitions of eating disorders and for improved methods to treat them. An even more
desirable goal would be to mount an effective effort to prevent
their occurrence in the first place by targeting young children
and adolescents who may be most at risk for these illnesses.

Megan's mother Diane highlights the need for effective prevention. "Back in the 1930s and '40s, teenagers started smoking cigarettes because they thought it was the cool thing to do.
At that point, there were no studies about the harmful effects
of smoking tobacco. But now we know better and warn our
kids about how hazardous smoking is. There have also been
effective ad campaigns aimed at kids to show them the dangers
of drinking alcohol and using drugs like ecstasy, cocaine, and
heroin. So why are we not warning the group at highest risk for

developing eating disorders—our teenagers—about how physically damaging and deadly these syndromes can be?"

Jody's mother Shirley further notes that the only time the media ever pays attention to eating disorders is if a celebrity is involved, like when Karen Carpenter died or when Princess Diana admitted she was bulimic, or, more recently, when Mary-Kate Olsen was diagnosed with an eating disorder. "It's not enough for the press that ordinary people struggle with these diseases every day," she says. "There always has to be a famous name attached before a story about eating disorders is deemed newsworthy and that's just not right. We need stories that reflect the realities of the disorders as well as ad blitzes along the lines of 'Friends Don't Let Friends Drive Drunk' to reach our kids before it's too late."

Chelsey's mother Donna adds, "Prevention efforts need to start in schools when kids are very young. Teaching self-esteem is the key. Children need to be taught to value themselves for who they are and for all of their talents. Dieting

"Children need to be taught to value themselves for who they are and for all of their talents."

is starting younger and younger these days. A friend of mine who is an elementary school teacher told me that girls in her third-grade class have brought cans of Slim-Fast to school for lunch. When my friend asked one of the students if her parents were aware that she was only having a diet drink for lunch, the little girl replied, 'Oh, sure. My mom's the one who gave it to me.' It's shocking. These kids are only seven or eight years old, they aren't even fully grown yet, and their parents are already filling their heads with the wrong ideas. I think all parents, and young mothers and fathers in particular, need to learn about nutrition and healthy lifestyle habits."

However, while very appealing to parents and professionals, the goal of preventing eating disorders is elusive. Certainly, educating the public about eating disorders and increasing broad public awareness—on the part not only of parents and children but also of teachers, counselors, and even medical professionals, such as pediatricians or other primary care physicians who may come into contact with young at-risk patients—of the dangers of these diseases can play a key role in their recognition and in preventing the first symptoms from turning into a full-blown disorder. At the same time, a vital component of the effort to prevent any disorder is a firm understanding of the risk factors that may contribute to its development. But in the case of eating disorders, that understanding is woefully incomplete. As discussed in Chapter 2, the causes of syndromes like anorexia nervosa and bulimia nervosa involve a mix of biological, environmental, psychological, and social factors whose exact contribution to the development of these disorders is not yet fully understood. To educate the public about the dangers of these disorders is one thing, but to effectively prevent their occurrence, especially in light of what little is known about their risk factors, is a much taller order. The programs that have been launched in an effort to prevent or at least reduce the occurrence of these disorders or their symptoms have been based on reasonable assumptions about dieting, body image, low self-esteem, and other elements implicated in the development of eating disorders, not on actual known truths about them. Some of these programs have shown promising results; most have met with only modest, if any, success.

This chapter examines some of the prevention approaches that have been tried, explores the controversial topic of whether treating obesity might be viewed as a risk factor for eating disorders, and offers tips on what parents and others can do themselves to help prevent eating disorders in children and adolescents.

Prevention Approaches

Two prevention approaches—"universal" and "targeted"—have been used to try to reduce the incidence of eating disorders. A universal prevention program is one that is applied to an entire group of people and is designed to prevent a disease before it begins by changing, at the group-wide level, the beliefs, attitudes, intentions, and behaviors associated with the occurrence of that disease. For example, people who smoke, eat foods high in fat and calories, and don't exercise are at risk of developing coronary heart disease (CHD).

A universal prevention program is one that is applied to an entire group of people and is designed to prevent a disease before it begins

A universal prevention program for CHD would provide education about the dangers of the disease (the single leading cause of death in the United States in 2004) as well as about the harmful effects of smoking, the benefits of eating well-balanced meals, and the need for moderate exercise regimens. Similarly structured, universal prevention approaches for eating disorders focus on an entire population, such as all the students in a high school or junior high school, to promote healthy weight regulation, discourage calorie-restrictive dieting (e.g., "crash" diets), and address the ways in which body image and eating are influenced by developmental, social, and cultural factors. Some universal prevention programs focus on broader issues, such as increasing self-esteem and social competence. By contrast, a targeted prevention program is one that tries to identify those individuals who are at high risk of developing eating disorders or who have already begun to exhibit symptoms. The individuals at high risk can be monitored carefully, and anyone who develops symptoms can be referred to treatment in an effort to eliminate the disorder before it becomes established.

For either a universal or targeted prevention method to succeed, risk factors need to be identified and then tested to determine whether their reduction actually decreases the occurrence of the disorder. So far, no risk factor for eating disorders has passed this test. And while some experts have argued that preventive activities should focus on those factors that may protect against the development of a disease (e.g., building higher levels of self-esteem), no studies have identified just what those "protective" factors are. There's also the question of how targeted prevention should accurately identify the high-risk individuals it is designed to monitor. Such an identification process would involve using a highly sensitive and specific screening tool to separate program participants into no-risk, high-risk, or case (those diagnosed with the disorder) groups, with the end result being that the high-risk group could receive targeted prevention and the case group could be referred for treatment. As yet, there is no such instrument that can satisfactorily separate individuals into these groups.

Given these circumstances, experts must rely on a limited number of studies to determine the effectiveness of current prevention methods aimed at reducing the incidence of eating disorders in children and adolescents.

Universal Prevention Programs in Schools

Most studies of universal prevention programs in schools have shown that these programs did increase knowledge and awareness of eating disorders, but were much less successful at changing attitudes and behavior. One study in 1997 even suggested that efforts at prevention may be counterproductive. Students who had recovered from an eating disorder shared their experiences with classmates and provided information about these diseases. During follow-up, it was found that those classmates who participated in the program had slightly *more* symptoms of eating disorders than those classmates who were not included in the program. More recent, better-developed programs suggest it may be possible to produce changes in attitudes about body shape and weight that persist for at least several months, but there is no evidence that such changes, in fact, have a significant impact in reducing the emergence of disturbed behaviors among students.

Disordered eating attitudes and behaviors can be difficult to change because they are often reinforced by a variety of family, peer, cultural, or other environmental factors. Consequently, some prevention researchers have argued for the need to systemically change the environment, particularly the school environment, of children and adolescents. One study in 1999 did demonstrate that system-wide changes in an elite ballet school reduced eating disorders in this high-risk setting. Another study, in 2000, focused on a community-based intervention that was designed to prevent disordered eating among preadolescent girls and that consisted of six 90-minute sessions emphasizing media literacy and advocacy skills. After three months, researchers found that the program did indeed have a positive influence on media-related attitudes and behaviors, including how the girls internalized sociocultural ideals. Unfortunately, few other studies have tested

. . . system-wide changes in an elite ballet school reduced eating disorders in this high-risk setting.

this prevention method in other environments, so it's hard to predict just how effective it might be in different settings.

Some experts have concluded that universal prevention programs are ineffective and should be abandoned altogether. But the truth, according to one analysis in 2002, is that the evidence does not "allow any firm conclusions to be made about the impact of prevention programs for eating disorders in children and adolescents." Many questions remain as to how to institute and better design universal prevention programs that have long-lasting impact on those adolescents who are at high risk of developing eating disorders. For example, what is the ideal age for such preventive interventions? How should environmental and family factors be included in these programs? Should universal prevention be provided to both boys and girls in the same setting? Until programs addressing such concerns are developed and allowed to run their course, the overall question of the effectiveness of universal prevention remains unanswered.

Targeted Prevention Programs in Schools

Most of the prevention programs that have targeted individuals who are at risk for eating disorders have focused on older adolescents or college students, and have shown some promising results, such as those reported in 1996. Researchers separated 315 at-risk female college students into two groups—a no-treatment group and a cognitive-behavioral therapy (CBT) group. After one month, the CBT group showed significant improvements in weight management behavior, body satisfaction, and self-esteem. These, and more clinically focused studies, show that intensive, targeted interventions can reduce risk factors, at least in the short term. However, as with the universal programs, no targeted programs are sufficiently well developed and of established effectiveness to suggest that they be widely employed. More study of this potentially important type of intervention is sorely needed.

Does the Treatment of Obesity Increase the Risk of Developing an Eating Disorder?

In *DSM-IV,* obesity is not considered an eating disorder or, more broadly, a mental disorder, but rather a general medical problem. Should its treatment be considered a risk factor for the development of eating disorders? This is a hot-button topic that has caused considerable controversy among eating disorders specialists and obesity experts. The presumed association between dieting and the development of symptoms of eating disorders has led school-based eating disorder prevention programs to warn students about the ill effects of dieting. Yet with obesity rapidly becoming a major public health problem for America's youth, it is important to understand whether treatments for obesity, specifically recommendations that restrict caloric intake, do in fact increase the risk for the development of eating disorders.

> The treatment of obesity . . . is a hot-button topic that has caused considerable controversy among eating disorders specialists and obesity experts.

Recent studies indicate that 16% of adolescents are overweight, a figure that has tripled since 1980. An additional 22% of adolescents are at risk of being overweight, compared to 15.7% in 1980. It is suspected that approximately 80% of overweight teenagers will become obese adults and will, as a result, experience increased risks of cardiovascular disease, high cholesterol, high blood pressure, diabetes mellitus, gallbladder disease, several cancers (e.g., breast and colon cancer), and psychosocial problems. Adults who were obese as teenagers suffer adverse health effects later in life, and obese teens are likely to suffer from health complications even before they reach adulthood. Type 2 ("adult onset") diabetes was once rare in children and adolescents, but recent reports show that one third of adolescents diagnosed with diabetes had the Type 2 form of the disease, which represents a ten-fold increase from rates in 1982, and diabetes may progress more quickly in youth than in adults.

A combination of reducing calories (i.e., dieting) and increasing physical activity is the cornerstone of weight management in overweight adolescents, just as it is in obese adults. However, some clinicians and researchers have been concerned that encouraging dieting may increase the risk of eating disorders, particularly among adolescent females, and that weight loss programs might do more harm than good. By contrast, obesity experts generally believe that early intervention during the adolescent period is the preferred method for dealing with obesity, citing the likelihood that a teen will receive family support and encouragement to lose weight, that eating habits and other behavior are more easily modified in a young person than they are in an adult, and that proliferation of fat tissue may be curtailed. Early treatment of obesity may also be cost-effective. By preventing overweight children and adolescents from becoming obese adults, health-care costs for treating obesity-related complications could be reduced.

Moreover, the vast majority of adolescent dieters *don't* develop eating disorders. Forty-four percent of teenage girls, by one estimate, report trying to lose weight, but the prevalence of eating disorders in females is only between 1% (anorexia nervosa) and

. . . the vast majority of adolescent dieters don't develop eating disorders.

3% (bulimia nervosa) and the rates among males are approximately one-tenth of those observed in females. Many more factors than simply attempting to diet contribute to the development of eating disorders. And while it's been proven that average-weight individuals do experience adverse behavioral and psychological effects from a severe restriction in calories, obese adults who have lost 10% of their initial body weight generally show improvements in mood and reductions in binge eating.

Weight Loss Interventions for Children and Adolescents

Effective strategies for overweight children and adolescents emphasize diet, physical activity, and behavioral changes. Dietary change may include reduced calorie and fat intake, or improved adherence to dietary guidelines, such as the Food Guide Pyramid produced by the Food and Nutrition Information Center, which offers healthy diets focused on needed nutrients as well as on caloric intake to maintain and improve weight. One well-studied approach to modifying the diets of young people is the Stoplight Diet, developed by obesity expert Dr. Leonard Epstein in the 1970s. The Stoplight Diet teaches children about nutrition by labeling foods according to traffic signals: High-calorie foods (like cookies and soda) are red and should be avoided, low-calorie foods (like most vegetables) are green and are okay to eat freely, and medium-calorie foods are yellow and can be consumed in moderation.

Other programs aimed at decreasing weight sensibly rely on increasing physical activity through aerobic exercise (e.g., swimming, jogging, or basketball) as well as through lifestyle changes that increase overall activity during daily routines (e.g., using stairs rather than elevators, walking instead of driving a short distance). Such programs also encourage the reduction of sedentary behaviors, such as watching television or playing video games. Preliminary studies have shown that changes in lifestyle activity have been more effective than structured exercise in maintaining weight loss.

. . . changes in lifestyle activity have been more effective than structured exercise in maintaining weight loss.

Parental involvement in the weight loss efforts of their children is also essential. For example, parents who modify their own eating or activity habits can encourage their children to follow suit. Additionally, parents can limit high-fat and high-sugar foods available at home while encouraging their children to eat fruits, vegetables, and other healthy choices. In fact, through these and other similar methods, parents can help children not only to lose as much as 25% of their weight but also to maintain their reduced weight for as long as ten years.

The Effects of Dieting and Weight Loss on Eating Behavior and Psychological Status

Most studies of the impact of well-developed weight loss programs —that is, those overseen by an experienced professional such as a physician, psychologist, or nutritionist—have found that children's preoccupation with dieting, unhealthy weight loss behaviors, and concerns about being overweight either decrease or stay the same, indicating that the weight loss efforts do not cause an increase in eating disorder symptoms.

For example, one study evaluated a program in which all participants followed the Stoplight Diet. Follow-up assessments, which were conducted 18 months after the completion of treatment, indicated that weight dissatisfaction, purging/restricting, and total symptoms of disordered eating showed no significant changes over time. Another study—one occurring over ten years, the longest to date—evaluated participants enrolled in one of four weight control programs during childhood. All of the interventions were family-based and used the Stoplight Diet. At reassessment, only 4% of the participants reported having been treated for bulimia nervosa over the course of the decade, and none reported being treated for anorexia nervosa.

These studies suggest that professionally administered weight loss programs pose minimal risks of precipitating eating disorders in overweight children and adolescents. Additional studies examining the relationship between dieting and binge eating support this view, indicating that diet programs do not appear to increase the occurrence of this behavior. Similarly, about half of adults with binge eating disorder report that dieting did not precede the onset of their disorder.

What about the effects of dieting and weight loss on a child's emotional state? Can these precipitate such emotional reactions as depression, anxiety, and irritability, as investigators worried some years ago? In research over the past decade, dieting has generally not been found to have a negative effect on mood. In one study, for example, participants lost an average of 20% of their weight while at the same time some aspects of their psychological status, such as social competence, improved. Another study found significant reductions in symptoms of depression and anxiety in children involved in a family-based weight control program.

> . . . dieting has generally not been found to have a negative effect on mood.

The Bottom Line on Obesity

Our current understanding that professionally administered weight loss programs for overweight children and adolescents do not increase eating disorder symptoms is based on a limited number of studies. Further research is needed to reconcile the consistent finding that dieting, as practiced in behavioral weight loss programs for overweight youngsters, appears associated with improved psychological and behavioral changes, with concerns that excessive dieting behavior can lead to an eating disorder. Several issues must be considered:

1. Healthy dieting, which encourages only modest caloric restriction, in combination with the increased consumption of low-fat dairy products and fruits and vegetables, appears to present few risks to overweight youth. By contrast, unhealthy weight loss behaviors, which include severe caloric restriction (e.g., crash diets) and the prohibition of certain foods (e.g., fad diets), could significantly increase the risk of eating disorders and emotional complications. This is possible in overweight youth, as well as in normal-weight adolescents, especially girls, who diet aggressively in pursuit of an ever-thinner ideal. Similarly, chronic restrained eating may pose risks that are not associated with healthy dieting.

2. Some overweight youth may be at risk for adverse behavioral consequences of dieting and weight loss even when they participate in a professionally administered program. Studies of individuals over many years, for example, have shown that severe body image dissatisfaction and weight and shape preoccupation are the most robust predictors of the development of eating disorders in adolescent girls. Thus, overweight teenagers with marked body image dissatisfaction, depression, or other psychiatric complications may be at greatest risk of

. . . overweight teenagers with marked body image dissatisfaction, depression, or other psychiatric complications may be at greatest risk of experiencing binge eating episodes

experiencing binge eating episodes when subjected to even modest caloric restriction.

3. Weight regain is common in overweight adolescents, as it is in obese adults. Studies of adults have not found weight cycling (i.e., weight loss followed by regain) to be associated with clinically significant behavioral consequences, but in overweight youth with a history of psychiatric complications, weight cycling might produce different effects. Whenever possible, follow-up assessment should be conducted through late adolescence when symptoms of bulimia nervosa or binge eating disorder might emerge.

Ultimately, large-scale trials are needed to determine the behavioral risks posed by different weight loss interventions for overweight youth. While health professionals, teachers, and parents will continue to be concerned about the all-too-common occurrence of misguided weight loss efforts among children and teenagers, all should be increasingly concerned about the growing epidemic of pediatric obesity. Sixteen percent of America's adolescents are already overweight and, as adults, will experience serious medical and psychosocial consequences from this condition. Concerns about the potential ill effects of dieting should not impede efforts to develop more effective methods of treating obesity among young people. Such concerns should also not discourage urgently needed efforts to prevent the development of excessive weight gain among both children and adults in the first place.

Perhaps, as in many areas of life, the best approach is one of *moderation*. Encouraging moderate, balanced food intake and moderate amounts of regular physical activity should be helpful in promoting a healthy lifestyle both for overweight youngsters and for those young people who tend toward the excessive caloric restriction and extreme exercise that are associated with eating disorders.

What Parents Can Do to Help Prevent Eating Disorders

The person who coined the phrase, "You can never be too rich or too thin," obviously hadn't witnessed someone struggling with the devastating effects of anorexia nervosa or another eating disorder. And yet, in a world where people are now more aware of eating disorders than they were 20 years ago, there is still a reverence for thinness. According to the National Eating Disorders Association, Americans spend more than $40 billion dollars annually on dieting and diet-related products, which is roughly equivalent to the amount the U.S. federal government spends on education each year.

It's no wonder the American people shell out so much money trying to become thinner, considering they're bombarded with images of skinny people at every turn. Excruciatingly thin models, actresses, actors, and athletes grace the covers of almost every magazine produced in this country (and in other industrialized nations as well) or are featured on the inside pages, where they hawk everything from clothing to perfume to personal hygiene products. And even if you don't buy such publications, your child is still exposed to them at every street-corner newsstand, in convenience stores, or next to grocery-store checkout counters, where it's nearly impossible to resist flipping through one while waiting in a long line. Images of rail-thin people are also plastered on huge billboards, on the sides of buses, in clothing-store windows, and in ads that pop up whenever you log onto the Internet. Television, however, takes the prize. During popular shows featuring female stars who appear to be significantly under-weight (e.g., the now-defunct *Ally McBeal*), TV networks sand-wich commercials for fast-food restaurants between ads for diets that promise incredible weight loss in very short periods of time.

The pervasive cultural message that to be attractive one must be thin, combined with the relentless promotion of dieting, provides a fertile environment in which eating disorders can take root in some people. What can you as a parent do to pre-vent the development of an eating disorder in your child? Where should you start? The National Eating Disorders Association recommends that the first thing you can do is to learn as much as you can about syndromes like anorexia nervosa, bulimia nervosa, and binge eating. By gaining genuine awareness, you can "avoid judgmental or mistaken attitudes about food, weight, body shape, and eating disorders."

It's equally important to examine both your own ideas and attitudes about your body and your behavior around your chil-dren. Do you make derogatory comments about your appear-ance in front of your daughter? Do you make disparaging remarks about the appearance of others while out with your son? Do you point out obese people to your child and say, "If you're not careful, you're going to look like that someday"? Do you ever gossip to your children about a friend or rela-tive looking awful because they're so fat? Such comments tell your kids that you value a person's appearance more than you do the person for who he or she is. Candy, who was obese as a teen but lost weight in her early twenties, offers an example of how much her mother's attitude affected her.

> It's . . . important to examine both your own ideas and attitudes about your body and your behavior around your children.

"My mom was very glamorous-looking in a 1940s movie-star sort of way. While I was growing up, all of my friends thought she was totally cool because she seemed so sophisticated and self-assured. What they didn't know was that every time she'd get dressed, she'd stand in front of the mirror and constantly put herself down because of her 'piano legs,' which was how she referred to her thick, stocky calves. She was so stunning that nobody else even noticed her legs, but all she could focus on was the one part of her body she felt made her imperfect. After constantly hearing her berate herself, I learned that there's always something—some part of you—that's unacceptable and makes you less of a person. Therefore, parents need to keep in mind that their kids are watching them and listening to everything they say about themselves and about others. If the comments are self-effacing or derogatory, children will assimilate those negative values."

". . . parents need to keep in mind that their kids are watching them and listening to everything they say about themselves and about others."

Another key element in the prevention of eating disorders is to make sure that you as a parent don't convey the message to your child that becoming thinner is a solution to all of life's challenges. Candy again:

"After I got really fat, my mom kept telling me that if I lost weight, I'd become the happiest girl in the whole USA. She swore that strangers on the street would stop and swoon as I walked by and boys at school would get into fights over who would take me out. In other words, in my mother's view, everything I ever dreamed of having could be attained if only I was thin. After I finally lost 100 pounds, which I did sensibly over a three-year period, I was totally crushed because it became clear that my mother was wrong. People didn't fall down on the street as I passed by, strangers didn't knock on my door to tell me how darned good I looked, and being thinner didn't help me achieve everything I'd hoped to in life."

If your child is overweight, don't tell her there's a pot of gold at the end of the weight loss rainbow. Instead, keep the expectations reasonable. Stress how much better she'll feel about herself or how much healthier she'll be if she loses weight. By presenting it in such a way, you let her know that it's more important to do something for herself rather than to please someone else or to be more attractive to another person. The same advice also applies if your child is a boy.

Along those same lines, Shirley speaks up about a dangerous trend rapidly spreading among teenagers in this country. "Two words: cosmetic surgery," she says. "I heard on the news that a girl received breast implants for her sixteenth birthday. When her parents came under fire for giving her such a gift, their explanation was they only did it because it was what she'd asked for. Can you imagine? Her breasts aren't even fully developed yet and they buy her implants? Those parents should be ashamed of themselves, as should the doctor who performed the procedure. So, too, should parents who allow their teenagers to have nose jobs, tummy tucks, or liposuction. We all know that adolescence is an awkward time physically, but these children aren't even allowing nature to take its course. They're having their bodies altered before they've had time to grow into them, with their parents obviously approving of it by footing the bills. If this trend keeps up, everybody will have cute perky noses, cute perky breasts, and cute perky butts. How boring is that? Don't these people understand that it's natural—and wonderful—to live in a world where everybody is different?"

Does your daughter comment about how she wishes she could look like everybody else? Has she internalized "thin ideals"? If you're unsure, sit down and talk to her. Find out how she feels about what she sees every day on TV, in magazines, and on the Internet. Donna regrets not having talked more with Chelsey, who read lots of fashion magazines and had a poster of the supermodel Kate Moss tacked up on her wall.

"I didn't think much about the poster at the time because Moss was very popular," she says. "She was constantly on TV and featured in hundreds of magazine ads. Having had pictures of movie stars and musicians on my wall while I was growing up, I figured Chelsey had the poster up because she liked Moss." It was only later, after her daughter was diagnosed with anorexia nervosa, that Donna discovered the real significance of Moss's presence in her daughter's room. It was Chelsey's reminder of what she thought she needed to look like to be attractive and successful and served as a triggering device to keep losing weight.

"The companies who used Moss in advertisements didn't think twice about what her image portrayed to young girls and women around the world. 'Be skinny and be a super-star.' I know my child suffered as a result of those advertisers' thoughtlessness, but corporations don't care about the harm they're doing as long as they continue to make money, so I've made a vow to not purchase any product that's promoted with the image of an emaciated-looking person. I've also told my relatives, friends, and neighbors to do the same. We need to band together to stop advertisements that can have disastrous effects on our children."

> "I've made a vow to not purchase any product that's promoted with the image of an emaciated-looking person."

Another necessary step toward the prevention of eating disorders is to educate teenagers about prejudice in its varying forms, including the bias against those who are overweight. If your son shows up one day wearing a "No Fat Chicks" t-shirt, it's definitely time for a heart-to-heart talk about the damage such an attitude can cause. The same response should be used if you hear your daughter talking to friends about how "fat and gross" a classmate is. Your children need to know that labeling people as "fat," "stupid," "geek," or "loser" serves no other purpose than to limit their opportunities to get to know people for who they really are.

Because eating disorders begin most frequently around puberty, it is essential to address the role of biology with your teen. A young girl who was formerly considered a "string bean" or a "tomboy" can suddenly become horrified by the fat that starts to grow around her hips, thighs, and buttocks. The development of breasts can also affect girls differently: Some are thrilled when their chests change while others are upset about it. Boys, too, can be resistant to the changes taking place in their bodies. Whatever the case with your child, be there and be supportive, but don't impose attitudes that he or she isn't yet ready for. Even if you think it's marvelous that your child is passing from childhood to adulthood, refrain from saying things like "Look at how wonderfully you're filling out," or "I can't believe how much my little boy has grown." While seemingly innocent enough, such remarks have the potential of increasing the self-consciousness some children already feel about their changing bodies or can cause them to take drastic measures (such as self-starvation or purging) in an attempt to battle the laws of nature. Instead, talk openly and honestly with them about what to expect in the near future (e.g., that gaining weight during puberty is natural, especially for girls), and be sure to let them know that it will be many years before their bodies stop growing and changing. If you're unsure of the actual biological facts or feel you need help with how best to discuss bodily changes with your teen, ask for advice from your child's pediatrician, your own doctor, or a health-education specialist.

In addition to the physical changes brought by the onset of puberty, your child faces emotional changes as well, which is why eating disorder specialists advise parents to discourage teasing someone about his or her appearance. It's true that playful teasing is part of family life; you've undoubtedly teased your children at some point, just as they've teased you. Still, if you laugh when your son calls his sister "thunder thighs" or when your daughter calls her brother "lard butt," your reaction can have a powerful negative impact on the child who's the brunt of the joke. Candy relates the following story:

"One day when I was about 15 and still really fat, I was walking through our living room when my brother said, 'Hey, you guys, where are you going?' I didn't really get it, but my mother started laughing hysterically. I finally figured out that he was making a joke about me being big enough to be two people. Since my brother was a stupid jerk, I could've easily blown him off if it hadn't been for the fact that my mother kept laughing. Not only that, but afterwards, she told everyone she knew—relatives, friends, neighbors, even people at her job— what my brother had said. Eventually, everybody started calling me 'you guys,' too. It was totally humiliating and I became very depressed. I mean, if your own mother doesn't mind you being ridiculed and even thinks it's funny, what can you expect from the rest of the world?" If your children tend to tease each other unmercifully about appearance, make a point of sitting down with each of them to explain how hurtful some jokes can be and why they should remember that people are more than just their bodies. Praise your kids for who they are and what they do, not how they look.

Have you ever told your children you can't go swimming with them because you'll "look like a beached whale" in your bathing suit? Have you avoided wearing shorts and sleeveless shirts because you don't want all of your "flab" hanging out? Do you wear high-heeled shoes because they make your legs look "longer" even as they hurt your feet? If you answered "yes" to any of the previous questions, you should stop and think about how your own attitudes and behaviors affect your teenagers. If you want them to be comfortable with their appearance, it is important that you show that you are comfortable with yours as well.

If your son or daughter is involved in a sport that requires a weight limit (i.e., gymnastics, ice skating, crew, or wrestling), talk to the coach about exactly what that weight limit is and ask if there's a structured nutritional program for your child to follow. As discussed in Chapter 4, many adolescents can become obsessed with pleasing teachers and coaches and often keep dropping pounds long after they've met the sport's required weight limit. By being informed about their training regimen, you won't be susceptible to excuses like "Coach says I need to lose a few more pounds," or "The teacher told me I shouldn't eat dinner because it will make me too fat for trials." Also, if you're worried that your child might be at particular risk of developing an eating disorder, it would be wise to suggest that he or she participate in a sport that doesn't involve being a certain size or shape. Cathleen did just that with her son Phil during his recovery from anorexia nervosa.

"After Phil returned to school, he was recruited for wrestling, but we nixed that idea big time because there would be too much pressure to weigh a certain amount and I didn't want Phil to start thinking he needed to lose weight again. Parents and coaches need to be on the same page about what's best for the child. Coaches who push too hard obviously don't realize how much influence they can have on an impressionable kid." When asked what she thought would help prevent eating disorders, Audra's mother Valerie said, "No school should have a weight limit for cheerleaders." While it's true that many cheerleading routines have become very complicated, with kids being thrown up into the air and squads standing on each other's shoulders, there should still be a place for everybody who wants to participate.

Megan's mother Diane suggests that one of the best ways to prevent eating disorders is to throw out your bathroom scale. "Kids with eating disorders become obsessed with the scale," she says. "Their days are dictated by how the numbers on that scale rise and fall. After Megan finally embraced recovery, the first thing I did was get rid of the scale and I also gave away all of our full-length mirrors. If you feel good about yourself and the way you look, there's no reason to have a mirror around so that you can fret about your image."

"... the first thing I did was get rid of the scale and I also gave away all of our full-length mirrors."

Other parents warn about the dangers of allowing your child access to everything that's posted on the World Wide Web. Since its inception, the Internet has become a vital tool for anyone seeking information that was formerly unavailable locally. Unfortunately, the downside is the number of Web sites that post things vulnerable teens shouldn't see. Parents of children with eating disorders mention this issue because, several years ago, personal Web sites promoting anorexia nervosa and bulimia nervosa as "lifestyles" and "choices" proliferated. These sites, dubbed "Pro-Ana" (pro-anorexia) and "Pro-Mia" (pro-bulimia), were created by individuals longing to make contact with others who had anorexia nervosa or bulimia nervosa. The sole purpose of this contact was to "chat" and "inspire" each other to continue the quest to be as thin as possible and/or to share tips about unhealthy behaviors like fasting or purging. Due to a huge public outcry about how harmful these sites can be, many have been shut down, yet some still remain and get daily hits from users all over the world. A recent post on one of the "Pro-Mia" sites was a question from someone who needed advice about where she could purge when the bathrooms at home were occupied. There were at least ten responses to the question, none of which told her she shouldn't make herself throw up in the first place. Instead, the answers offered suggestions as to where she could vomit without being caught and how to get rid of the evidence later. Such posts make it obvious that people in the throes of eating disorders still do visit existing "Pro-Ana" and "Pro-Mia" sites on a regular basis. If you believe your child is susceptible to developing an eating disorder or is recovering from one, it would be wise to block access to such sites on all of the computers in your home, just as you would block hard-core porn sites. If you have qualms about censorship, keep in mind that as a parent you are responsible for protecting your child from anything you deem harmful. As one mother said, "You wouldn't let your kid stand in front of an oncoming car or allow them to put their hand over an open flame, so why would you let them have access to Web sites that could trigger disordered eating behavior or, worse, prove fatal?"

If you want to learn more about the prevention of eating disorders, there are numerous national organizations you can contact, many of which are listed in the Resources section of this book.

Chapter Six

Conclusion: A Call for Action

I n the last several years, public concern about eating disorders has prompted legislative action at national and state levels. On February 26, 2003, the Eating Disorders Coalition (EDC), whose mission is to advance the federal recognition of eating disorders as a public health priority, sponsored a congressional briefing in Washington, DC, entitled "When Kids Can't Concentrate: How Eating Disorders Impact Our Children." During the briefing, Representative Judy Biggert (R-IL) announced to a group of over 55 activists that she and Representative Ted Strickland (D-OH) had introduced the bipartisan Eating Disorders Awareness, Education, and Prevention Act of 2003 (H.R. 873) in the U.S. House of Representatives.

The bill amends the Elementary and Secondary Education Act of 1965 to authorize the use of innovative assistance funds for programs that would (1) improve identification of students with eating disorders; (2) increase awareness of such disorders among parents and students; and (3) train educators with respect to effective eating disorders prevention assistance. It also directs the Secretary of Education to carry out a program to broadcast public service announcements to improve public awareness and to promote the identification and prevention of eating disorders. Additionally, it requires the National Center for Education Statistics and the National Center for Health Statistics to (1) study the impact eating disorders have on educational advancement and achievement; (2) report on current state and local programs to educate youth on the dangers of eating disorders; and (3) recommend federal, state, and local measures that could be undertaken.

During the briefing, the mother of not one but two daughters with eating disorders spoke eloquently and passionately about the impact these illnesses have had on her family and why there is an urgent need for the passage of such a bill. She described the years of grueling struggle with "this monster we call ED," the long nights she spent by her daughters' "bedsides making sure they keep breathing," and in fact the relentless vigilance that was required 24/7 to keep her children alive. The control ED had over her first daughter "was bigger than anything we were prepared for and we watched helplessly as she cycled through treatment facilities, with her insurance company making decisions that jeopardized her recovery and her life. What she must have suffered is unimaginable and incomprehensible. Her anguish and pain were overwhelming and, on several occasions, she tried to end that pain." When her second daughter was hit with the disease, she "succumbed so rapidly and severely" and her health "became so medically compromised" that without immediate medical treatment she would die. "All of your waking hours," this mother said, "are spent searching for treatment facilities that will take her while all of your 'attempting to sleep' time is spent by her bedside making sure she continues to breathe."

Addressing the financial impact of these illnesses, she said, "My husband and I have exhausted all financial resources to help our children. The average length of treatment has been 60 days at a cost of $30,000 per month. You can do the math; we choose not to. Our 401k's are a thing of the past, we have remortgaged the house, taken

"My husband and I have exhausted all financial resources to help our children."

out loans, and maxed out all our credit cards. But we are ready to do even more if we have to.

"We are all exhausted emotionally and physically. Neither of my daughters has been able to complete [her] education. My youngest has totally relapsed and is back in treatment. She can't even finish her freshman year of college. And as for my oldest, she is in recovery, but there is not a day that goes by when she doesn't suffer from the ramifications of her eating disorder. She has chronic stomach problems, irritable bowel syndrome from years of laxative abuse, recurring headaches from repeated over-doses of prescription drugs, and fibromyalgia, to name but a few of her physical complications. At 23 years of age, she is in constant pain and yet works aggressively on her goal of one day being able to get her college degree, which is no longer a given but something she will have to fight very hard for."

For all the wrenching emotional, physical, and financial hardships that eating disorders have visited upon her family, she told the briefing, "I have never lost hope. I believe there are choices to make: We can concentrate on the pain itself or we can allow the pain to drive our passion to make a difference. I think the choice is obvious. We need policies that recognize eating disorders as serious threats to our children. We desperately need funding and resources for education, treatment, and prevention. We have run out of time. This is a matter of life and death, but I refuse to even think about the prospect of having to start a foundation in memory of my daughters. My

children, your children, deserve a future and we have an obligation and a responsibility to secure it for them."
As of this writing, H.R. 873 has yet to pass.

As was discussed in Chapter 3, the Mental Health Parity Act of 1996 mandated companies with more than 50 employees to eliminate annual and lifetime dollar limits for the treatment of mental illnesses. Regrettably, many states found loopholes allowing them to place new restrictions on mental health benefits. In response, the Senator Paul Wellstone Mental Health Equitable Treatment Act (S. 486 and H.R. 953) was introduced both in the U.S. Senate and in the U.S. House of Representatives in February 2003. If passed, the bill, in short, would prohibit certain employee group health plans or related insurances from imposing limitations on mental health treatment, with certain exclusion conditions. As the EDC states, "For people with eating disorders, mental health parity is a matter of life or death" and therefore it is "vital to ban insurance discrimination against people with mental health disorders." (More information about this bill, and about HR 873, can be found on the EDC's Web site, www.eatingdisorderscoalition.org.)

Many states don't have treatment facilities that provide comprehensive care for people with eating disorders, and even when care is available, many families cannot afford it due to inadequate insurance coverage. On Monday, June 21, 2004, Governor George Pataki signed into law a bill that provides funding for Comprehensive Care Centers for Eating Disorders in New York State. The law (Article 27-J) authorizes $1.5 million per year to fund three centers providing necessary services, such as inpatient treatment, rehabilitation and psychiatric care, and prevention and research activities, among other things. (Complete guidelines for the New York program can be found at www.health.state.ny.us.) This is an impressive effort by New

York State to assure improved treatment for its citizens with eating disorders. If successful, it may become a model for similar efforts across the country.

In addition to legislative changes to assure that families can obtain the help they require, research is desperately needed to understand the social, psychological, and biological causes of eating disorders and to develop more effective methods of treatment. The current lack of understanding about the fundamental disturbances that lead to eating disorders and about how to prevent them demands support for more research.

Last, as individuals and as a nation we must work to decrease the stigma, secrecy, and shame that accompany eating disorders so that those in need of treatment will seek it. The parents quoted in this book have all, in their own ways, become powerful advocates for children and adolescents with eating disorders. Some have done so publicly, by speaking at conferences and giving talks around the country about the dangers of eating disorders, by helping to establish charitable foundations dedicated to advancing the knowledge and treatment of these disorders, and by forming support groups in their local community. Others have taken a more private route, working on behalf of their own children by fighting tirelessly to get them the right treatment and to help them along the long road to recovery. And all of course have shared their experiences in this book in order to offer their practical wisdom about these illnesses to you.

. . . as individuals and as a nation we must work to decrease the stigma, secrecy, and shame that accompany eating disorders . . .

Whether in small steps or large strides, all of these parents, and thousands of others whose children have been affected by these disorders, are helping to lift the silence and stigma that surround these illnesses and to change our nation's cultural and political climate so that real progress in the diagnosis, treatment, and prevention of these complex illnesses can be made. Eating disorders, as one mother put it in Chapter 4, are first and foremost "family diseases." They are also syndromes with an increasing prevalence among our young people, and as a result there are many families like your own who are dealing with them every day. You and your child are not, in short, alone in your struggle to beat these illnesses. Reach out and get help. Get support from others whose lives have been touched by eating disorders, find out about the ongoing research on these disorders by consulting with qualified professionals, educate yourself about available treatments, read other books besides just this one—in short, stay informed about every aspect of your child's illness and recovery, and most important, don't give up until he or she is safely out of harm's way. You can also help your own family and others like yours by advocating for improved health care coverage and for more research on eating disorders. You *can* make a difference, and your child will surely benefit from your efforts in the long run.

Glossary

acute treatment Any treatment that is aimed at achieving rapid reduction of symptoms.

amenorrhea The absence of menstrual periods.

anticonvulsant A medication that helps prevent seizures. Many anticonvulsants have mood-stabilizing effects as well.

antidepressant A medication used to prevent or relieve depression.

antipsychotic A medication used to prevent or relieve psychotic symptoms. Some newer antipsychotics have mood-stabilizing effects as well.

anxiety disorder Any of several mental disorders that are characterized by extreme or maladaptive feelings of tension, fear, or worry.

atypical antipsychotic One of the newer antipsychotic medications. Some atypical antipsychotics are also used as mood stabilizers.

bipolar disorder A mood disorder characterized by an overly high mood, called mania, which alternates with depression. Also called manic depression.

body mass index (BMI) A measure of weight relative to height (calculated as weight in kilograms divided by height in meters squared. A calculator is at http://nhlbisupport.com/bmi/bmicalc.htm).

celiac disease A digestive disorder that can result in weight loss and malnutrition.

cognitive-behavioral therapy (CBT) A form of psychotherapy that aims to correct ingrained patterns of thinking and behavior that may be contributing to a person's mental, emotional, or behavioral symptoms.

comorbidity The simultaneous presence of two or more disorders.

cortisol A hormone released by the adrenal glands that is responsible for many of the physiological effects of stress.

depression A feeling of being sad, hopeless, or apathetic that lasts for at least a couple of weeks. See major depression.

diabetes   A disease marked by high levels of sugar in the blood (hyperglycemia), which can be caused by too little insulin (a hormone produced by the pancreas to regulate blood sugar), resistance to insulin, or both.

Diagnostic and Statistical Manual of Mental Disorders, **Fourth Edition**, **Text Revision** (*DSM-IV*)   A manual that mental health professionals use for diagnosing all kinds of mental illnesses.

diuretic   Any substance that causes increased production of urine.

eating disorder   A disorder characterized by serious disturbances in eating behavior. People may severely restrict what they eat, or they may go on eating binges, then attempt to compensate by such means as self-induced vomiting or misuse of laxatives.

electrolytes   Salt constituents (sodium, potassium, chloride, and bicarbonate) found naturally in the bloodstream that are needed to maintain normal functions.

family therapy   Psychotherapy that brings together several members of a family for therapy sessions.

group therapy   Psychotherapy that brings together several patients with similar diagnoses or issues for therapy sessions.

hospitalization   Inpatient treatment in a facility that provides intensive, specialized care and close, round-the-clock monitoring.

hyperthyroidism   Overactive thyroid.

hypothalamus   Part of the brain that serves as the command center for the nervous and hormonal systems.

individual therapy   Psychotherapy in which a patient meets one-on-one with a therapist.

inflammatory bowel disease   A general term for diseases (for example, Crohn's disease and ulcerative colitis) that cause inflammation in the intestines/digestive tract.

interpersonal therapy (IPT)   A form of psychotherapy that aims to address the interpersonal triggers for mental, emotional, or behavioral symptoms.

ipecac   A substance used to induce vomiting after accidental poisoning.

laxative   A substance that helps promote bowel movements.

maintenance therapy   Any treatment that is aimed at preventing a recurrence of symptoms.

major depression   A mood disorder that involves either being depressed or irritable nearly all the time, or losing interest or enjoyment in almost everything. These feelings last for at least two weeks, are associated with several other symptoms, and cause significant distress or impaired functioning.

Medicaid   A government program, paid for by a combination of federal and state funds, that provides health and mental health care to low-income individuals who meet eligibility criteria.

menarche   The first occurrence of menstruation during puberty.

mental health parity   A policy that attempts to equalize the way that mental and physical illnesses are covered by health plans.

mental illness   A mental disorder that is characterized by abnormalities in mood, emotion, thought, or higher-order behaviors, such as social interaction or the planning of future activities.

monoamine oxidase inhibitor (MAOI)   An older class of antidepressant.

mood   A pervasive emotion that colors a person's whole view of the world.

mood disorder   A mental disorder in which a disturbance in mood is the chief feature. Also called affective disorder.

mood stabilizer   A medication for bipolar disorder that reduces manic and/or depressive symptoms and helps even out mood swings.

neurotransmitter   A chemical that acts as a messenger within the brain.

obsessive-compulsive disorder (OCD)   A mental disorder that is characterized by being obsessed with a certain idea and/or feeling compelled by an urgent need to engage in certain rituals.

partial hospitalization   Services such as individual and group therapy, special education, vocational training, parent counseling, and therapeutic recreational activities that are provided for at least 4 hours per day.

pathology   An abnormal condition or biological state in which proper functioning is prevented.

perfectionism   A feeling that anything less than perfect is unacceptable.

personality disorders   A constellation of personality traits that significantly impair one's ability to function socially or cause personal distress.

pituitary gland   A small gland located at the base of the brain. Its hormones control other glands and help regulate growth, metabolism, and reproduction.

placebo   A sugar pill that looks like a real medication, but does not contain an active ingredient.

postmenarcheal   After the onset of menstruation.

prevalence   The total number of cases of a disease existing in a given population at a given point in time or during a specified time.

Pro-Ana/Pro-Mia   Terms used to describe Web sites that promote anorexia nervosa/bulimia nervosa as "lifestyles" and "choices" rather than as disorders or illnesses.

protective factor   A characteristic that decreases a person's likelihood of developing an illness.

psychiatrist   A medical doctor who specializes in the diagnosis and treatment of mental illnesses and emotional problems.

psychologist   A mental health professional who provides assessment and therapy for mental and emotional disorders. Also called a clinical psychologist.

psychosocial   Any situation in which both psychological and social factors are assumed to play a role.

psychotherapy   The treatment of a mental, emotional, or behavioral disorder through "talk therapy" and other psychological techniques.

purging   In the case of eating disorders, purging means to rid oneself of food eaten, either via self-induced vomiting or by using laxatives, diuretics, or enemas.

randomized controlled trial   A study in which participants are randomly assigned to a treatment group or a control group. The control group typically receives either a placebo or standard care. This study design allows researchers to determine which changes in the treatment group over time are due to the treatment itself.

recurrence   A repeat episode of an illness.

relapse   The reemergence of symptoms after a period of remission.

remission   A return to the level of functioning that existed before an illness.

residential treatment center   A facility that provides round-the-clock supervision and care in a dorm-like group setting. The treatment is less specialized and intensive than in a hospital, but the length of stay is often considerably longer.

reuptake   The process by which a neurotransmitter is absorbed back into the sending branch of the nerve cell that originally released it.

risk factor   A characteristic that increases a person's likelihood of developing an illness.

schizophrenia   A severe form of mental illness characterized by delusions, hallucinations, or serious disturbances in speech, behavior, or emotion.

selective serotonin reuptake inhibitor (SSRI)   A widely prescribed class of antidepressant.

serotonin   A neurotransmitter that plays a role in mood and helps regulate sleep, appetite, and sexual drive.

side effect   An unintended effect of a drug.

sociocultural   Involving both social and cultural factors.

substance abuse   The continued use of alcohol or other drugs despite negative consequences, such as dangerous behavior while under the influence or substance-related personal, social, or legal problems.

subtype   A group that is subordinate to a larger type or class.

suicidality   Suicidal thinking or behavior.

targeted prevention program   A program that tries to identify those who are at high risk of developing a disorder or those who have already begun to exhibit symptoms.

temperament   A person's inborn tendency to react to events in a particular way.

tricyclic antidepressant (TCA)   An older class of antidepressant.

Type 2 diabetes   See diabetes mellitus.

universal prevention program   A program intended to benefit an entire group of people, not just those identified as being at risk for developing a disorder.

Resources

Books and Other Materials

Berg, Francis M. *Underage and Overweight: America's Childhood Obesity Epidemic—What Every Parent Needs to Know.* New York: Hatherleigh Press, 2004.

Dying to Be Thin. NOVA/PBS documentary originally broadcast on December 12, 2000, which can be viewed free online by logging on to www.pbs.org/wgbh/nova/thin/program.html

Herrin, Marcia, and Nancy Matsumoto. *The Parent's Guide to Childhood Eating Disorders: A Nutritional Approach to Solving Eating Disorders.* New York: Owl Books, 2002.

Hirschmann, Jane, and Lela Zaphiropoulos. *Preventing Childhood Eating Problems.* Carlsbad, CA: Gurze Books, 1993.

Kater, Kathy. *Real Kids Come in All Sizes: Ten Essential Lessons to Build Your Child's Body Esteem.* New York: Broadway, 2004

Lock, James, and Daniel Le Grange. *Help Your Teenager Beat an Eating Disorder.* New York: Guilford Press, 2005.

Lucas, Alexander R. *Demystifying Anorexia Nervosa: An Optimistic Guide to Understanding and Healing.* New York: Oxford University Press, 2004.

Natenshon, Abigail H. *When Your Child Has an Eating Disorder: A Step-by-Step Workbook for Parents and Caregivers.* San Francisco: Jossey-Bass, 1999.

Richardson, Brenda Lane, and Elane Rehr. *101 Ways to Help Your Daughter Love Her Body.* New York: HarperCollins, 2001.

Sherman, Roberta Trattner, and Ron A. Thompson. *Bulimia: A Guide for Friends and Family.* San Francisco: Jossey-Bass, 1996.

Siegel, Michele, Judith Brisman, and Margot Weinshel. *Surviving an Eating Disorder: Strategies for Family and Friends,* rev. ed. New York: HarperPerennial, 1997.

Teachman, Bethany A., Marlene B. Schwartz, Bonnie S. Gordic, and Brenda S. Coyle. *Helping Your Child Overcome an Eating Disorder: What You Can Do at Home.* Oakland: New Harbinger Publications, 2003.

Resources for Information, Support, and/or Treatment Referrals

Note: If you do not have access to the Internet in your home, visit your local public library, which likely has computers and Internet access that will enable you to browse the Web sites listed here. In most public libraries, this service is free of charge.

Academy for Eating Disorders (AED)
60 Revere Drive, Suite 500
Northbrook, IL 60062-1577
(847) 498-4274
www.aedweb.org

Alliance for Eating Disorders Awareness
P.O. Box 13155
North Palm Beach, FL 33408-3155
(866) 662-1235
info@eatingdisorderinfo.org

American Academy of Child and Adolescent Psychiatry
3615 Wisconsin Avenue N.W.
Washington, DC 20016-3007
(202) 966-7300
www.aacap.org

American Academic of Pediatrics (AAP)
141 Northwest Point Boulevard
Elk Grove Village, IL 60007-1098
(847) 434-4000
www.aap.org

American Association of Suicidology
4201 Connecticut Avenue N.W., Suite 408
Washington, DC 20008
(202) 237-2280
www.suicidology.org

American Foundation for Suicide Prevention
120 Wall Street, 22nd Floor
New York, NY 10005
(888) 333-2377
www.afsp.org

American Obesity Association
1250 24th Street, N.W., Suite 300
Washington, DC 20037
(202) 776-7711
www.obesity.org

American Psychiatric Association
1000 Wilson Boulevard, Suite 1825
Arlington, VA 22209-3901
(703) 907-7300
www.psych.org

American Psychological Association
750 First Street N.E.
Washington, DC 20002-4242
(800) 374-2721
www.apa.org

Anorexia Nervosa and Related Eating Disorders, Inc. (ANRED)
603 Stewart Street
Seattle, Washington 98101
(800) 931-2237
www.anred.com

Bazelon Center for Mental Health Law
1101 15th Street N.W., Suite 1212
Washington, DC 20005
(202) 467-5730
www.bazelon.org

Center for the Study of Anorexia and Bulimia
A Division of the Contemporary Institute for Psychotherapy
1841 Broadway, 4th Floor
New York, NY 10023
(212) 333-3444
www.csabnyc.org

Center for Young Women's Health—Children's Hospital Boston
333 Longwood Avenue, 5th Floor
Boston, MA 02115
(617) 355-2994
www.youngwomenshealth.org

Centers for Medicare and Medicaid Services
7500 Security Boulevard
Baltimore, MD 21244-1850
(877) 267-2323 (toll free) or (410) 786-3000 (Baltimore, MD)
www.cms.hhs.gov

Depression and Related Affective Disorders Association
2330 W. Joppa Road, Suite 100
Lutherville, MD 21093
(410) 583-2919
www.drada.org

Eating Disorders Anonymous
Meetings are held in 27 states nationwide. Contact information can be found at
www.eatingdisordersanonymous.org

Eating Disorders Association (EDA)
103 Prince of Wales Road
Norwich NR1 1DW
United Kingdom
0870-770-3256
www.edauk.com

Eating Disorders Coalition (EDC)
611 Pennsylvania Avenue S.E. #423
Washington, DC 20003-4303
(202) 543-9570
www.eatingdisorderscoalition.org

Eating Disorders Referral and Information Center
(800) 843-7274 (for therapist referrals)
www.edreferral.com

Eating Disorders Research Unit
Columbia University Medical Center
New York State Psychiatric Institute
1051 Riverside Drive

New York, NY 10032
(212) 543-5739
www.eatingdisordersclinic.org

Food and Drug Administration
5600 Fishers Lane
Rockville, MD 20857
(888) 463-6332
www.fda.gov

Food and Nutrition Information Center
Agricultural Research Service, USDA
National Agricultural Library, Room 105
10301 Baltimore Avenue
Beltsville, MD 20705-2351
(301) 504-5719
www.nal.usda.gov/fnic/

Gurze Books Eating Disorders Resources
P.O. Box 2238
Carlsbad, CA 92018
(800) 756-7533
www.gurze.com

Harvard Eating Disorders Center
55 Fruit Street, YAW 6900
Boston, MA 02114
(617) 726-8470
www.hedc.org

International Association of Eating Disorders Professionals (IAEDP)
P.O. Box 1295
Pekin, IL 61555-1295
(800) 800 8126
www.iaedp.com

Lifelines Foundation for Eating Disorders
600 Lake Air Drive, Suite #9A
Waco, TX 76710
(254) 741-9998
www.lfed.org

National Alliance for the Mentally Ill
Colonial Place Three

2107 Wilson Boulevard, Suite 300
Arlington, VA 22201-3042
(800) 950-6264
www.nami.org

National Association of Anorexia Nervosa and Associated Disorders (ANAD)
P.O. Box 7
Highland Park, IL 60035
(847) 831-3438
www.anad.org

National Centre for Eating Disorders
54 New Road
Esher, Surrey KT10 9NU
United Kingdom
0845-838-2040
www.eating-disorders.org.uk

National Eating Disorders Association (NEDA)
603 Stewart Street, Suite 803
Seattle, WA 98101
(800) 931-2237
www.nationaleatingdisorders.org

National Eating Disorder Information Centre—Canada (NEDIC)
ES 7-421, 200 Elizabeth Street, M5G 2C4
Toronto, Canada
(866) 633-4230 (toll free in Canada) or (416) 340-4156 (Toronto)
www.nedic.ca

National Eating Disorders Screening Program
Screening for Mental Health
One Washington Street, Suite 304
Wellesley Hills, MA 02481
(781) 239-0071
www.mentalhealthscreening.org

National Institute of Clinical Excellence (NICE)
MidCity Place, 71 High Holborn
London WC1V 6NA
United Kingdom
0207-067-5800
www.nice.org.uk

National Institute of Diabetes and Digestive and Kidney Diseases (NIDDK)
National Institutes of Health
Office of Communications and Public Liaison
Building 31, Room 9A04 Center Drive, MS 2560
Bethesda, MD 20892-2560
www.niddk.nih.gov

National Institute of Mental Health
Office of Communications
6001 Executive Boulevard, Room 8184, MSC 9663
Bethesda, MD 20892-9663
(866) 615-6464
www.nimh.nih.gov

National Institute of Nutrition
Canadian Council of Food and Nutrition
3800 Steeles Avenue West, Suite 301A
Woodbridge, Ontario L4L 4G9
(905) 265-9124
www.nin.ca

National Institutes of Health
9000 Rockville Pike
Bethesda, MD 20892
(301) 946-4000
www.nih.gov
(Numerous toll free phone numbers can be found on the NIH Information
Lines Web page at www.nih.gov/health/infoline.htm)

National Mental Health Association
2001 N. Beauregard Street, 12th Floor
Alexandria, VA 22311
(800) 969-6642
www.nmha.org

National Mental Health Information Center
Substance Abuse and Mental Health Services Administration
P.O. Box 42557
Washington, DC 20015
(800) 789-2647
www.mentalhealth.org

National Women's Health Information Center/Office on Women's Health
8550 Arlington Boulevard, Suite 300

Fairfax, VA 22031
(800) 994-9662; (888) 220-5446 for the hearing impaired
www.4woman.gov
(A companion page for girls can be found by logging on to www.4girls.gov.)

Society of Adolescent Medicine (SAM)
1916 Copper Oaks Circle
Blue Springs, MO 64015
(816) 224-8010
www.adolescenthealth.org

Something Fishy
www.something-fishy.org
A Web site that describes its mission as "dedicated to raising awareness and
providing support to people with eating disorders and their loved-ones."

United States Department of Health and Human Services—Substance Abuse
and Mental Health Services Administration (SAMHSA) National Mental
Health Information Center
P.O. Box 42557
Washington, DC 20015
(800) 789-2647; (866) 889-2647 for the hearing impaired; (240) 747-5484 for
international calls
www.mentalhealth.org

Yale Center for Eating and Weight Disorders
P.O. Box 208205
New Haven, CT 06520-8205
(203) 432-4610
www.yale.edu/ycewd/

Bibliography

American Psychiatric Association. *Diagnostic and Statistical Manual of Mental Disorders* (4th ed., text revision). Washington, DC: American Psychiatric Association, 2000.

Evans, Dwight L., and Linda Wasmer Andrews. *If Your Adolescent Has Depression or Bipolar Disorder: An Essential Resource for Parents.* New York: Oxford University Press with the Annenberg Foundation Trust at Sunnylands and the Annenberg Public Policy Center at the University of Pennsylvania, 2005.

Evans, Dwight L., Edna B. Foa, Raquel E. Gur, Herbert Hendin, Charles P. O'Brien, Martin E. P. Seligman, and B. Timothy Walsh. *Treating and Preventing Adolescent Mental Health Disorders: What We Know and What We Don't Know—A Research Agenda for Improving the Mental Health of Our Youth.* New York: Oxford University Press with the Annenberg Foundation Trust at Sunnylands and the Annenberg Public Policy Center at the University of Pennsylvania, 2005.

Lock, James, and Daniel Le Grange. *Help Your Teenager Beat an Eating Disorder.* New York: Guilford Press, 2005.

Lock, James, Daniel Le Grange, Stewart Agras, and Christopher Dare. *Treatment Manual for Anorexia Nervosa: A Family-Based Approach.* New York: Guilford Press, 2001.

Lucas, Alexander R. *Demystifying Anorexia Nervosa: An Optimistic Guide to Understanding and Healing.* New York: Oxford University Press, 2004.

Natenshon, Abigail H. *When Your Child Has an Eating Disorder: A Step-by-Step Workbook for Parents and Other Caregivers.* San Francisco: Jossey-Bass, 1999.

Ryan, Joan. *Little Girls in Pretty Boxes: The Making and Breaking of Elite Gymnasts and Figure Skaters.* New York: Doubleday, 1995.

Siegel, Michele, Judith Brisman, and Margot Weinshel. *Surviving an Eating Disorder: Strategies for Family and Friends.* New York: Perennial Library, 1988.

Walsh, B. Timothy. "Eating Disorders." In D. L. Kasper, E. Braunwald, A. S. Fauci, S. L. Hauser, D. L. Longo, and J. L. Jameson (eds.): *Harrison's Principles of Internal Medicine* (16th ed.). New York: McGraw Hill, in press.

Walsh B. Timothy. "Eating Disorders." In A. Tasman, J. Kay, and J. A. Lieberman (eds.): *Psychiatry* (2nd ed.). London: Wiley, 2003.

Index

academic goals, 129
academic pressure, 3
academic services, 72
activities, participation in, 126
Adolescent Mental Health Initiative, 6
adult onset diabetes, 141. *See also* diabetes
adults, 105–6, 114–18. *See also* coaches; parents; teachers
advertisements, 151
affective disorders, 48
Ally McBeal (television show), 148
amenorrhea, 15, 26, 27, 29, 54. *See also* menstruation
American Academy of Child and Adolescent Psychiatry, 92
American Academy of Pediatrics, 30, 33, 64, 65
American Journal of Psychiatry, 22
American Psychiatric Association, 12
amitriptyline. *See* Elavil
Anafranil (clomipramine), 86–87, 92
Annenberg Foundation Trust, 6
annual dollar limits, 160. *See also* costs
anorexia nervosa, 8–11; diagnosis of, 12–15, 30; medical complications of, 52–55; prevalence of, 4–6, 9–10; psychological treatments for, 83–84; relapse prevention and, 94–97; symptoms of, 14–15. *See also* bulimia; eating disorders
anticonvulsants, 89
antidepressants, 86–88, 90–91, 92, 97, 98
anti-obesity agents, 89
anxiety disorders, 48, 70, 87, 90
appearance, 3, 45, 126, 154
Asian American students, 36
athletes, 24
Ativan (lorazepam), 90
attention span, 9, 54

atypical antipsychotics, 88
avoidant personality disorders, 49

bathroom scales, 155
behavioral problems, 91
Biggert, Judy, 157
binge eating, 4, 68, 79, 121, 145; diagnosis and, 15, 17, 20–22, 27–29, 35, 56; hospitalization and, 69. *See also* bulimia nervosa; purging
binge eating disorder, 20–22, 29, 144–46
binge-eating/purging type (AN-B/P), 15, 27–28, 50. *See also* anorexia
bipolar disorder, 88
birth control, 91
blackouts, 14, 106
black students, 35
bloating, 53
blood cell count, 53
blood pressure, 141
body image, 69, 135–36, 145
body mass index (BMI), 35
body shape, 18, 21, 24, 28–29, 44–45, 79–80
body size, 116
body temperature, 53
bone development, 52, 53–55
borderline personality disorders, 49
brain chemistry, 38–39
brain function, 53
brain tumors, 32
breast development, 152. *See also* puberty
bulimia nervosa, 16–20; medical complications of, 55–56; prevalence of, 4–6; psychological treatments for, 84–85; relapse prevention and, 97–98; symptoms of, 19–21. *See also* anorexia; eating disorders

About the Authors

B. Timothy Walsh, MD is Ruane Professor of Pediatric Psychopharmacology in the College of Physicians & Surgeons at Columbia University and founder of the Eating Disorders Research Unit at the New York State Psychiatric Institute. He was chair of the Adolescent Mental Health Initiative's formal Commission on Eating Disorders, a blue ribbon panel of leading authorities convened in 2003 to assess the current research on these disorders; the findings of Dr. Walsh's commission make up the scientific foundation of this book.

V. L. Cameron is a freelance writer based in New York City.

BASEMENT